George William Marshall

Parish Registers

A List of those Printed, or of Which ms. Copies Exist in Public Collections...

George William Marshall

Parish Registers

A List of those Printed, or of Which ms. Copies Exist in Public Collections...

ISBN/EAN: 9783337254919

Printed in Europe, USA, Canada, Australia, Japan

Cover: Foto ©ninafisch / pixelio.de

More available books at **www.hansebooks.com**

TOGETHER WITH

References to Extracts therefrom, Printed and Manuscript.

BY

GEORGE W. MARSHALL.

PRIVATELY PRINTED.

1891.

PREFACE.

THE following references are an amplification of a reply made a few years since to an inquiry of the late editor of the 'Genealogist,' Mr. Walford D. Selby, as to what Parish Registers had been printed. It is almost needless to say that this list might be much extended, especially were indexes to the MS. collections of Genealogical Antiquaries remaining in the British Museum and other public libraries to any appreciable extent contributed to it. As it stands it is, I believe, the only attempt which has been made to arrange in alphabetical order a list of Registers and Register Extracts which are readily available for the use of genealogists, and which, in many cases, may save them the trouble of making an original search, or a tedious and expensive journey to some country parish.

It is well to state what sources have been examined for the compilation of this catalogue, and the plan which has been followed in selecting the references. Only *general* extracts are noticed. When those relating only to one family are given, I have not referred to them, because so far as printed works are concerned reference to my 'Genealogists' Guide' will usually give a clue. I think I can fairly claim to have included all, or very nearly all, the Registers which have been printed *in extenso* as separate works, as well as those of which there are MS. copies in the British Museum and Herald's College. Amongst the principal books from which extracts are noted are the 'Collectanea Topographica et Genealogica,' 'Reliquary,' 'Genealogist,' 'Miscellanea Genealogica et Heraldica,' Blades' 'Genealogia Bedfordiensis,' Harvey's 'Hundred of Willey,' Malcolm's 'Londinum

Redivivum,' 'Notes and Queries,' 'The East Anglian,' Nichols' 'Topographer,' etc.

I have experienced great difficulty in determining how many extracts from a Register should entitle it to a reference in these pages, and have been unable to decide upon any general rule. In some few instances only half a dozen may be found. If those who consult this calendar deem any of my references frivolous, I shall be glad to hear their objections, and to consider how far I can amend my ways should this preliminary list become the precursor of a more extensive work.

Most of the references to MSS. are to the collection of the late Colonel Chester, now remaining in the College of Arms. I cannot pass over so important a collection as this without making some remarks upon it, and the way I have dealt with its contents. The Colonel was an omnivorous genealogist who assimilated everything in the likeness of a Register, good, bad, or indifferent, which came in his way; now copying wholesale from the contents of printed books, and again transferring to his volumes the labours of others whose MSS. he had borrowed. In many counties he probably had not made a single original search. The result, however, was eminently satisfactory, for he succeeded in getting into his hands, by these means, a far more extensive collection than would have been possible had he worked, so to speak, single-handed. In the MS. collections transferred to his pages will be found, no doubt with some exceptions, those of Rawlinson from his MSS. in the Bodleian, Mr. Arthur Staunton Larken's and Lord Monson's for Lincolnshire, the Rev. Frederick Brown's for Somersetshire, portions of the Davy MSS. in the British Museum; and among those genealogists who afforded him matter from their collections may be mentioned Sir Albert W. Woods, Garter, G. E. Cokayne, Norroy King of Arms, A. S. Gatty, York Herald, J. Paul Rylands, the Rev. J. Ingle Dredge, Rev. C. H. Mayo, R. Garraway Rice, E. J. Sage, and F. Grigson.

I have been able to detect a good deal of copying from printed books, and there is, probably, much more than I am learned enough

in topographical literature to identify. Whenever I have been able
to identify this form of piracy, I have carefully omitted any reference
to Colonel Chester's transcript, giving reference only to the printed
book. I may add that I shall be much obliged to anyone who will
point out to me any extracts in print which I have here calendared
as part of this MS. collection, in order that they may be added in a
future edition instead of the references to the Colonel's MSS. Before
laying down my pen, I must write my apology for sending to the
press an index of which no one knows better than I do the incom-
pleteness. It is but an attempt to lay the foundation of what I hope,
as years roll on, may be developed by other hands than mine into a
comprehensive guide to that literature of Parish Registers which is
daily growing in importance. It is the first attempt of a working-
man to help his fellows, and as such, I trust, merits consideration
though it needs correction.

GEORGE W. MARSHALL.

A GUIDE TO PARISH REGISTERS.

ABBOTSHAM. Chester MSS. in Coll. Arms, (Devon,) iv. 187-215.
ABBOTS' LANGLEY. Chester MSS. in Coll. Arms, (Herts,) ii. 197.
ABENHALE. MS. in Coll. Arms, R. B. G. xxxviii. 7.
ABINGDON, ST. HELEN'S. Chester MSS. in Coll. Arms, (Berkshire,) 21-61.
ABINGTON PIGOTTS. The Parish Registers of Abington Pigotts, 1653-1812. Edited by W. G. F. Pigott, Rector. Norwich, 1890, 4to.
ACKWORTH. 1558-1599. Yorkshire Notes and Queries, i. 108-118, 166-173.
ADDERBURY. Chester MSS. in Coll. Arms, (Oxfordshire,) i. 235.
ADDINGTON, GREAT. MS. in Coll. Arms, R. B. G. xxiii. 126.
       „   LITTLE. MS. in Coll. Arms, R. B. G. xxiii. 127.
       „   Collectanea Topographica et Genealogica, vii. 286.
Church Notes and Registers, MS. in Coll. Arms, 24.
ADWELL. Chester MSS. in Coll. Arms, (Oxfordshire.) ii. 257.
AISTHORPE. Chester MSS. in Coll. Arms, (Lincolnshire,) i. 207.
ALBURY. Chester MSS. in Coll. Arms, (Oxfordshire,) i. 191.
ALCESTER. Excerpta ex Registris Parochialibus in Com. Gloucester. Middle Hill, 1854, fol.
ALCONBURY-CUM-WESTON. Chester MSS. in Coll. Arms, (Hunts,) 1.
ALDBOROUGH. Chester MSS. in Coll. Arms, (Yorkshire,) ii. 207.
ALDBOURN. Collectanea Topographica et Genealogica, vi. 385.
ALDENHAM. Chester MSS. in Coll. Arms, (Herts,) ii. 31-90.
ALDERBURY, (co. Wilts). Original Register, 1606-1669. British Museum, Add. MS. 27441.
ALDERTON. MS. in Coll. Arms, R. B. G. xxxviii. 16.
ALDWINCLE, ALL SAINTS'. Chester MSS. in Coll. Arms, (Northampton,) ii. 1-24.
       „   ST. PETER. Chester MSS. in Coll. Arms, (Northampton,) ii. 25-55.
ALFORD. Chester MSS. in Coll. Arms, (Lincolnshire,) iv. 293.
ALKERTON. Chester MSS. in Coll. Arms, (Oxfordshire,) i. 207.
ALLERSTON. See EBBERSTON.
ALMER. MS. in Coll. Arms, J. P. cxcii. 304.

ALNWICK. MS. in Coll. Arms, C. G. Y. 186, p. 127. Chronicon Mirabile, or Extracts from Parish Registers, 136.

ALREWAS Chester MSS. in Coll. Arms, (Staffordshire,) 89.

ALTHORPE. Chester MSS. in Coll. Arms, (Lincolnshire,) ii. 5.

ALTON PANCRAS. Chester MSS. in Coll. Arms, (Dorset.) 71.

ALVASTON. Chester MSS. in Coll. Arms, (Derbyshire,) i. 1.

ALVERSTOKE. Chester MSS. in Coll. Arms, (Hants.) 109-124.

ALVESCOTT. Chester MSS. in Coll. Arms, (Oxfordshire,) ii. 261.

ALVESTON. Excerpta ex Registris Parochialibus in Com. Gloucester. Middle Hill, 1854, fol. MS. in Coll. Arms, R. B. G., xxxviii. 15. Chester MSS. in Coll. Arms, (Warwickshire,) 279.

ALVINGHAM. Chester MSS. in Coll. Arms, (Lincolnshire,) i. 171.

ALWINGTON. Complete transcript, Marriages and Baptisms, 1550-1716 ; Burials, 1550-1775. Chester MSS. in Coll. Arms, (Devon,) i. 57-74 ; v. 1-89.

AMBERLEY. Chester MSS. in Coll. Arms, (Sussex,) i. 9, 53.

AMBROSDEN. Chester MSS. in Coll. Arms, (Oxfordshire,) ii. 263.

AMPTHILL. Blades' Genealogia Bedfordiensis, 1.

ANDERBY. Chester MSS. in Coll. Arms, (Lincolnshire,) i. 344.

ANDERSTONE. MS. in Coll. Arms, J. P. cxcv. 75.

APPLEBY. Chester MSS. in Coll. Arms, (Lincolnshire,) i. 338.

APPLEBY MAGNA. The Reliquary, xii. 139.

ARDINGLEY. Chester MSS. in Coll. Arms, (Sussex,) i. 306.

ARDLEY. Chester MSS. in Coll. Arms, (Oxfordshire,) i. 215.

,, (co. Herts). New England Historical and Genealogical Register, xl. 274-280.

ARKSEY. British Museum, Add. MSS. 24469, 24572. Chester MSS. in Coll. Arms, (Yorkshire,) ii. 341.

ARLESEY. Blades' Genealogia Bedfordiensis, 6.

ARLINGHAM. Chester MSS. in Coll. Arms, (Gloucestershire,) 29-50. MS. in Coll. Arms, R. B. G. xxxviii. 5.

ARMTHORPE. British Museum, Add. MS. 24469.

ARNOLD. Chester MSS. in Coll. Arms. (Notts.) ii. 58.

ASHBOURNE. The Reliquary, xxv. 177, 241 ; xxvi. 42, 69, 156. Chester MSS. in Coll. Arms, (Derbyshire,) i. 169-270.

ASHBURNHAM Chester MSS. in Coll. Arms, (Sussex,) i. 370.

ASHBURTON. Chester MSS. in Coll. Arms, (Devon,) i. 171.

ASHBY-CUM-FENBY. Chester MSS. in Coll. Arms, (Lincolnshire,) iii. 402.

ASHFORD-IN-THE-WATER. The Reliquary, ii. 155.

ASHLEY. Hare's Miscell. Par. Registers, MS. in Coll. Arms, 141. MS. in Coll. Arms, R. B. G. xxiii. 106.

ASHPRINGTON. Chester MSS. in Coll. Arms, (Devon,) i. 15.

ASHTED. MS. in Coll. Arms, J. P. 193, 279.

ASHTON-UNDER-HILL. Excerpta ex Registris Parochialibus in Com. Gloucester. Middle Hill, 1854, fol. MS. in Coll. Arms, R. B. G. xxxviii. 15.

ASKERSWELL. Chester MSS. in Coll. Arms, (Dorset,) 207.

ASLACKBY. Chester MSS. in Coll. Arms, (Lincolnshire,) i 312

ASPLEY-GUISE. Blades' Genealogia Bedfordiensis, 8.

ASTHALL. Chester MSS. in Coll. Arms, (Oxfordshire,) ii. 269.

ASTON CLINTON. Chester MSS. in Coll. Arms, (Bucks,) 147.

ASTON-JUXTA-BIRMINGHAM. Registers from the year 1600-1637. Midland Antiquary, Vol. i., pp. 24, 69, 123 ; Vol. ii., pp. 15, 75 ; Vol. iii., p. 131 ; Vol. iv. 29, 63, 148.

ASTON ROWANT. Chester MSS. in Coll. Arms, (Oxfordshire,) ii. 277.

ASTON-SUB-EDGE. Collectanea Topographica et Genealogica, vii. 279. Chester MSS. in Coll. Arms, (Gloucestershire,) 153.

ASTWICK. Blades' Genealogia Bedfordiensis, 11.

ATTENBOROUGH-CUM-BRAMCOTE. The Reliquary, xii. 33, 105 ; xiii. 75.

AUKLAND, ST. ANDREW. Chronicon Mirabile, or Extracts from Parish Registers, 12.

     ,,   ST. HELEN. Chronicon Mirabile, or Extracts from Parish Registers, 22.

AUSTERFIELD. British Museum, Add. MS. 24596.

AUTHORPE. Chester MSS. in Coll. Arms, (Lincolnshire,) i. 351.

AVELEY. Original (Bishops') transcripts, 1636-1813. British Museum, Add. MS. 28737.

AWRE. MS. in Coll. Arms, R. B. G. xxxviii. 4.

AYCLIFFE. Chronicon Mirabile, or Extracts from Parish Registers, 36.

AYLESBY. Chester MSS. in Coll. Arms, (Lincolnshire,) iv. 1.

AYLESHAM. Hare's Miscell. Par. Registers, MS. in Coll. Arms, 163.

AYOTT, ST. LAWRENCE. Chester MSS. in Coll. Arms, (Herts.) ii. 25.

     ,,   ST. PETER. Church Notes and Registers. MS. in Coll. Arms, 12.

BABRAHAM. The East Anglian, ii. 218.

BACKFORD. Collectanea Topographica et Genealogica, iv. 232.

BADGWORTH. MS. in Coll. Arms, R. B. G. xxxviii. 18 b.

BADMINTON. MS. in Coll. Arms, R. B. G. xxxviii. 2.

BADSEY. Excerpta ex Registris Parochialibus in Com. Gloucester. Middle Hill, 1854, fol. Chester MSS. in Coll. Arms, (Worcestershire,) 249.

BAKEWELL. The Reliquary, v. 73.

BALDOCK. Chester MSS. in Coll. Arms, (Herts,) ii. 91.

BALDWIN BRIGHTWELL. Chester MSS. in Coll. Arms, (Oxfordshire,) i. 75.

BALSCOTT. Chester MSS. in Coll. Arms, (Oxfordshire,) ii. 295.

BALSHAM. Parish Registers. MS. in Coll. Arms, E. L. xi. 87.

BAMBROUGH. MS. in Coll. Arms, C. G. Y. clxxxvi. 134. Chronicon Mirabile, or Extracts from Parish Registers, 118.

BAMPTON (co. Oxon). MS. in Coll. Arms, J. P. cxcii. 384.

BANBURY. Chester MSS. in Coll. Arms, (Oxfordshire,) i. 167-190.

BANSTEAD. Chester MSS. in Coll. Arms, (Surrey.) iii. 159-198.

BANWELL. Complete copy, 1568-1797. Chester MSS. in Coll. Arms, (Somerset,) ii. 307-400 ; iii. 1-33, 61-118.

BARDNEY. Chester MSS. in Coll. Arms, (Lincolnshire,) ii. 141.

BARDWELL. Chester MSS. in Coll. Arms, (Suffolk,) 189.

BARFORD, GREAT. Blades' Genealogia Bedfordiensis, 12.
   „   LITTLE. Blades' Genealogia Bedfordiensis, 16.
BARKHAM. Chester MSS. in Coll. Arms, (Berkshire,) 91.
BARKING. Notes and Queries, 3 S. ii 343 ; iii. 283. Chester MSS.
   in Coll. Arms, (Essex.) i. 28-143.
BARKSTONE. Chester MSS. in Coll. Arms, (Lincolnshire,) i. 336.
BARLING. Original (Bishop's) transcripts, 1768. British Museum,
   Add. MS. 32344.
BARLINGS. Chester MSS. in Coll. Arms, (Lincolnshire,) iv. 37.
BARMBY UPON-DUN. Historical Notices of Doncaster, by C. W. Hat-
   field, 3 Series, 37. British Museum, Add. MS. 21469.
BARNARD CASTLE. Chronicon Mirabile, or Extracts from Parish
   Registers, 40.
BARNES. Chester MSS. in Coll. Arms, (Surrey,) i. 299-354.
BARNOLDBY-LE-BECK. Chester MSS. in Coll. Arms, (Lincolnshire,)
   iv. 5.
BARNSLEY. Chester MSS. in Coll. Arms, (Yorkshire,) ii. 377.
BARNSTON. The Genealogist, v. 23.
BARRINGTON. Chester MSS. in Coll. Arms, (Somerset,) i. 309.
   „   PARVA. MS. in Coll. Arms, R. B. G. xxxviii. 20.
BARROW. Chester MSS. in Coll. Arms, (Lincolnshire,) i. 201.
   „   Chester MSS. in Coll. Arms, (Suffolk), 317.
   „   GURNEY. Chester MSS. in Coll. Arms, (Somerset,) i. 25.
BARROW-CUM-TWYFORD. The Reliquary. i. 231.
BARTON, ST. PETER. Chester MSS. in Coll. Arms, (Lincolnshire,) i.
   41.
   „   ST. MARY. Chester MSS. in Coll. Arms, (Lincolnshire,) i.
   47.
BARTON-LE-CLEY. Blades' Genealogia Bedfordiensis, 18.
BARTON-ON-HUMBER. Chester MSS. in Coll. Arms, (Lincolnshire),
   v. 279
BASCHURCH. The Reliquary, vi. 19.
BASFORD. Chester MSS. in Coll. Arms, (Notts,) ii. 60.
BASILDEN. Parish Registers, MS. in Coll. Arms, E. L. xi. 18.
BASSINGTHORPE-CUM-WESTBY. Chester MSS. in Coll. Arms, (Lin-
   colnshire,) i. 26 ; v. 369.
BATCOMBE. Chester MSS. in Coll. Arms, (Somerset,) i. 261.
BATLEY. Chester MSS. in Coll. Arms, (Yorkshire.) ii. 325.
BATH, ABBEY. The Genealogist, New Series, vi. 92, 183. Parish
   Registers, MS. in Coll. Arms, R. B. G. xxii. 165 ; xxiv. 17.
BATH, ST. JAMES. MS. in Coll. Arms, R. B. G. xxiv. 42.
BATTLESDEN. Blades' Genealogia Bedfordiensis, 21.
BAUMBER. Chester MSS. in Coll. Arms, (Lincolnshire,) ii. 134.
BEACHAMPTON. Chester MSS. in Coll. Arms, (Bucks,) 141.
BECKENHAM Chester MSS. in Coll. Arms, (Kent,) i. 23-48. Church
   Notes and Registers, MS. in Coll. Arms, 18.
BECKFORD. Excerpta ex Registris Parochialibus in Com. Gloucester.
   Middle Hill, 1854, fol. MS. in Coll. Arms, R. B. G. xxxviii.
   11.
BECKINGHAM. Chester MSS. in Coll. Arms, (Lincolnshire,) ii. 246.

BEDDINGHAM. Chester MSS. in Coll. Arms, (Sussex,) i. 21.
BEDFORD, ST. CUTHBERT. Blades' Genealogia Bedfordiensis, 23.
  „ ST. JOHN. Blades' Genealogia Bedfordiensis, 24
  „ ST. MARY. Blades' Genealogia Bedfordiensis, 25.
  „ ST. PAUL. Blades' Genealogia Bedfordiensis, 34.
  „ ST. PETER-MARTIN. Blades' Genealogia Bedfordiensis, 40.
Chester MSS. in Coll. Arms, (Bedfordshire,) 379.
BEDINGHAM. The East Anglian, iv. 270.
BEDWYN MAGNA. Collectanea Topographica et Genealogica, v. 28.
  „ PARVA. Collectanea Topographica et Genealogica, v. 361.
BEELSBY. Chester MSS. in Coll. Arms, (Lincolnshire.) iv. 9.
BEESBY-IN-THE-MARSH. Chester MSS. in Coll. Arms, (Lincolnshire.)
ii. 30.
BEGBROOKE. Chester MSS. in Coll. Arms, (Oxfordshire,) i. 259.
BELLEAU. Chester MSS. in Coll. Arms, (Lincolnshire,) i. 341.
BELTON (IN AXHOLME). Chester MSS. in Coll. Arms, (Lincolnshire,)
i. 30.
BENGEWORTH. Excerpta ex Registris Parochialibus in Com. Glou-
cester. Middle Hill, 1854, fol.
BERE REGIS. Chester MSS. in Coll. Arms, (Dorset,) 201.
BERKELEY. MSS. in Coll. Arms, R. B. G. xxii. 145 ; xxxviii. 24.
Chester MSS. in Coll. Arms, (Somerset,) i. 119.
BERKHAMPSTEAD, ST. PETER. Church Notes and Registers, MS. in
Coll. Arms, 13.
BERMUDA, ST. GEORGE. Miscellanea Genealogica et Heraldica, New
Series, iv. 182, 202, 208, 319, 326.
BERWICK-ON TWEED. MS. in Coll. Arms, C. G. Y. clxxxvi. 142.
Chronicon Mirabile, or Extracts from Parish Registers, 110.
BEVERLEY, ST. MARY. Chronicon Mirabile, or Extracts from Parish
Registers, 144.
BEVERSTON. Chester MSS. in Coll. Arms, (Gloucestershire,) 281.
BEXLEY. The Genealogist, New Series, i. 58, 112, 224.
BICESTER. Chester MSS. in Coll. Arms, (Oxfordshire,) i. 1-17.
BIDDENHAM. Blades' Genealogia Bedfordiensis, 43. Harvey's Hun-
dred of Willey, 27.
BIDEFORD. MS. in Coll. Arms, J. P. cxcii. 204.
BIDFORD. Chester MSS. in Coll. Arms, (Warwickshire,) 101.
BIGGLESWADE. Blades' Genealogia Bedfordiensis, 47.
BILLINGBOROUGH. Chester MSS. in Coll. Arms, (Lincolnshire,)
ii. 164 ; v. 321.
BILLINGHAM. Chronicon Mirabile, or Extracts from Parish Registers,
26.
BILLINGHAY. Chester MSS. in Coll. Arms, (Lincolnshire,) ii. 294 ;
v. 337.
BILLINGTON. Blades' Genealogia Bedfordiensis, 46.
BILSBY. Chester MSS. in Coll. Arms, (Lincolnshire,) iii. 386.
BINGHAM. Chester MSS. in Coll. Arms, (Notts,) ii. 98.
BIRCHAM NEWTON. The Parish Register of Bircham Newton, Nor-
folk, 1562-1743. Edited by Richard Howlett. Norwich, 1888, 8vo.
BIRDBROOK. Chester MSS. in Coll. Arms. (Essex.) i. 20.

BIRMINGHAM, ST. MARTIN'S. The First Register Book of St. Martin, Birmingham, 1554-1653. Walsall, 1889, 8vo. Midland Antiquary, iii. 67.

BIRSTALL. British Museum, Add. MS. 24600. Yorkshire Notes and Queries, i. 25. Parish Registers, MS. in Coll. Arms, E. L. xi. 88.

BISHAMPTON. Excerpta ex Registris Parochialibus in Com. Gloucester. Middle Hill, 1854, fol.

BISHOP MIDDLEHAM. Chronicon Mirabile, or Extracts from Parish Registers, 31.

BISHOP NORTON. Chester MSS. in Coll. Arms, (Lincolnshire,) ii. 17.

BISHOPSBOURNE. Chester MSS. in Coll. Arms, (Kent,) i. 91.

BISHOPS' CLEEVE. Chester MSS. in Coll. Arms, (Gloucestershire,) 1.

BISHOPS' HULL. Chester MSS. in Coll. Arms, (Somerset,) iii. 185.

BISHOPS' LAVINGTON. The Genealogist, New Series, iv. 68.

BISHOPWEARMOUTH. Chronicon Mirabile, or Extracts from Parish Registers, 72.

BISLEY. MS. in Coll. Arms, R. B. G. xxxviii. 3.

BLACKBURTON. Chester MSS. in Coll. Arms, (Oxfordshire,) ii. 307.

BLADON. Chester MSS. in Coll. Arms, (Oxfordshire,) i. 271 ; iii. 337.

BLACKFORD. Chester MSS. in Coll. Arms, (Somerset,) ii. 19.

BLECHINGDON. Chester MSS. in Coll. Arms, (Oxfordshire,) i. 273.

BLETCHINGLEY. Chester MSS. in Coll. Arms, (Surrey,) iv. 255.

BLETSOE. Blades' Genealogia Bedfordiensis, 48. Harvey's Hundred of Willey, 497.

BLUNHAM. Blades' Genealogia Bedfordiensis, 50. Chester MSS. in Coll. Arms, (Bedfordshire,) 25.

BLYBOROUGH. Chester MSS. in Coll. Arms, (Lincolnshire,) i. 66.

BLYTON. Chester MSS. in Coll. Arms, (Lincolnshire,) i. 205.

BOBBINGTON. Original (Bishops') transcripts, 1662-1812. British Museum, Add. MS. 28738.

BOBBINGWORTH. The Parish Registers of Bobbingworth, Essex. Baptisms, 1559-1782 ; Marriages, 1559-1753 ; Burials, 1558-1785. Privately printed for Frederick Arthur Crisp. 1884, fol. Extracts from 1538, Church Notes and Registers, MS. in Coll. Arms, 11.

BOLDRE. MS. in Coll. Arms, J. P. cxciii. 476.

BOLINGBROKE. Chester MSS. in Coll. Arms, (Lincolnshire,) i. 13 ; ii. 123.

BOLNHURST. Blades' Genealogia Bedfordiensis, 53.

BOLTON (co. Lanc.). Bolton Parish Registers, 1573-1712. Printed in Bolton Weekly Journal.

BOSTON. Chester MSS. in Coll. Arms, (Lincolnshire,) iii. 181, 198, 285.

BOTTESFORD. Chester MSS. in Coll. Arms, (Lincolnshire,) ii. 9, 382.

BOTUS FLEMING. Heraldic Church Notes from Cornwall, by A. J. Jewers, 158.

BOURN. Chester MSS. in Coll. Arms, (Lincolnshire,) i. 370.

BOXLEY. Original (Bishops') transcripts, 1585-6, 1599-1600. British Museum, Add. MS. 32344.

BOX 7 BRO

BOXTED. Chester MSS. in Coll. Arms, (Suffolk,) 341.
BOYTON. East Anglian, iv. 217.
BRACEBOROUGH. Chester MSS. in Coll. Arms, (Lincolnshire,) ii. 24.
BRACEBRIDGE. Chester MSS. in Coll. Arms. (Lincolnshire.) i. 250.
BRADFIELD. British Museum, Add. MS. 24568. 'Bradfield, Berks, and Wolvercote, Oxon. Notes from the Parish Registers.' Oxford, 1888, 8vo.
BRADFORD. Complete Transcript, 1559-1812. Chester MSS. in Coll. Arms, (Devon,) ii. 291-381.
BRADFORD (co. York). A Copy of Buriall Register of Bradford Parish Church. Begins October 1, 1596. The Bradford Antiquary, pp. 46, 102, 160, 227. (In progress.)
BRADLEY. Chester MSS. in Coll. Arms, (Lincolnshire,) iv. 15.
BRAILSFORD. Chester MSS. in Coll. Arms, (Derbyshire,) i. 379.
BRAMCOTE. Chester MSS. in Coll. Arms, (Notts,) ii. 287.
BRAMLEY. Chester MSS. in Coll. Arms, (Yorkshire.) ii. 315.
BRAMPTON. British Museum, Add. MS. 24569. MS. in Coll. Arms, R. B. G. xxiii. 131.
BRANCEPATH. Chronicon Mirabile, or Extracts from Parish Registers 24.
BRANSCOMBE. MS. in Coll. Arms, J. P. cxcii. 234.
BRAUNTON. Chester MSS. in Coll. Arms, (Devon,) i. 11.
BREIGHTON. British Museum, Add. MS. 24572.
BRETFORTON. Excerpta ex Registris Parochialibus in Com. Gloucester. Middle Hill, 1851, fol. Marriages at Bretforton, co. Worcester, 1538-1752. London, 1831, 8vo. Printed by Sir Thomas Phillipps, Bart.
BREWOOD. Chester MSS. in Coll. Arms, (Staffordshire,) 31.
BRIDGNORTH, ST. LEONARD. Original (Bishops') transcripts, 1636-1812. British Museum, Add. MS. 28735.
„ ST. MARY MAGDALEN. Original (Bishops') transcripts, 1662-1813. British Museum, Add. MS. 28736.
BRIDGWATER. Chester MSS. in Coll. Arms, (Somerset,) i. 171.
BRIGSLEY. Chester MSS. in Coll. Arms, (Lincolnshire,) iii. 395.
BRIGSTOCK. Chester MSS. in Coll. Arms, (Northampton,) i. 1-21.
BRIMPSFIELD. Gloucestershire Notes and Queries, i. 402, 459.
BRINGTON. Chester MSS. in Coll. Arms, (Northampton.) i. 23-46.
BRISTOL, ST. NICHOLAS. Chronicon Mirabile, or Extracts from Parish Registers, 141.
BRIXWORTH. MS. in Coll. Arms, R. B. G. xxiii. 130.
BRIZE NORTON. Chester MSS. in Coll. Arms, (Oxfordshire,) i. 289.
BROAD CHALKE. Registers of Broad Chalke, Wilts, 1538-1780. Edited by Rev. C. G. Moore. London, 1880, 8vo.
BROADWATER. Chester MSS. in Coll. Arms, (Sussex,) i. 335.
BROADWAY. Baptisms and Burials from Broadway Register in various years, 1680-1771. Printed by Sir Thomas Phillipps, N.D. pp. 16. 12mo. Chester MSS. in Coll. Arms, (Worcestershire,) 301-372.
BROADWELL. MS. in Coll. Arms, R. B. G. xxxviii. 19.

BROADWINDSOR. Chester MSS. in Coll. Arms, (Dorset,) 223.

BROCKENHURST. MS. in Coll. Arms, J. P. cxciii. 496.

BROMHAM. Blades' Genealogia Bedfordiensis, 55. Harvey's Hundred of Willey, 71.

BROMLEY. Chester MSS. in Coll. Arms, (Kent,) i. 49-90. Church Notes and Registers, MS. in Coll. Arms, 19.

BROMSGROVE. Bromsgrove Church its History and Antiquities, by W. A. Cotton, 133.

BROOKLAND. Original (Bishops') transcripts, 1615. British Museum, Add. MS. 32344.

BROSELEY. The Parish Registers of Broseley, 1570-1750. Edited by A. F. C. C. Langley. London, 1889-90, 8vo. 2 vols.

BROUGHTON (co Northampton). MS. in Coll. Arms, R. B. G. xxiii. 129.

BROXBOURNE. Chester MSS. in Coll. Arms, (Herts.) ii. 10.

BRUNDISH. The Parish Registers of Brundish, Suffolk. Baptisms, 1562-1765; Marriages, 1563-1749; Burials, 1563-1785. Privately printed for F. A. Crisp. 1885, fol.

BRUTON. Chester MSS. in Coll. Arms, (Somerset,) i. 127.

BRYANSTON. Chester MSS. in Coll. Arms, (Dorset,) 217.

BUCKINGHAM. Chester MSS. in Coll. Arms, (Bucks,) 77-123.

BUCKLAND. (1551-1804, apparently a complete copy.) Excerpta ex Registris Parochialibus in Com. Gloucester. Middle Hill, 1854, fol.

BUCKLAND NEWTON. Chester MSS. in Coll. Arms, (Dorset,) 243.

BULWICK. Chester MSS in Coll. Arms, (Northampton,) i. 71-87.

BUNBURY. Chester MSS. in Coll. Arms, (Cheshire,) 301.

BURBAGE. Collectanea Topographica et Genealogica, vii. 180.

BURES. Chester MSS. in Coll. Arms, (Suffolk,) 15.

BURFORD. Chester MSS. in Coll. Arms, (Oxfordshire,) ii. 1.

BURFORD (co Salop). The Genealogist, ii. 353.

BURGH (near Aylsham). The Register of the Parish of Burgh, 156°-1810. By Rev. E. T. Yates. Printed in Proceedings of Norfolk and Norwich Archaeological Society, and separately, 8vo.

BURGH-IN-THE-MARSH. Chester MSS. in Coll. Arms, (Lincolnshire,) i. 156; ii. 377.

BURGH, ST. PETER. East Anglian, i. 268.

BURNESTON. Chester MSS. in Coll. Arms, (Yorkshire,) ii. 363.

BURNHAM. Collectanea Topographica et Genealogica, iv. 286. Church Notes and Registers, MS. in Coll. Arms, 5.

BURTON-BY-LINCOLN. Chester MSS. Coll. Arms, (Lincolnshire,) i. 10; iv. 67; v. 183.

BURWELL. Chester MSS. in Coll. Arms, (Lincolnshire,) i. 111.

BURY ST. EDMUND, ST. JAMES. Chester MSS. in Coll. Arms, (Suffolk,) 177.

     ,,   ,,   ST. MARY. Chester MSS. in Coll. Arms, (Suffolk), 181.

CADDINGTON. Blades' Genealogia Bedfordiensis, 58. Church Notes and Registers, MS. in Coll. Arms, 2.

CAISTOR. Chester MSS. in Coll. Arms, (Lincolnshire,) ii. 311; v. 1.

CALCEBY. Chester MSS. in Coll. Arms, (Lincolnshire,) i. 247.

CALVERLEY. The Registers of the Parish Church of Calverley in the co. of York, 1574-1720. By Samuel Margerison. Bradford, 1880-1887, 3 vols. 8vo.

CAM. Chester MSS. in Coll. Arms, (Gloucestershire,) 271.

CAMBERWELL. Collectanea Topographica et Genealogica, iii. 142. Church Notes and Registers, MS. in Coll. Arms, 25.

CAMBRIDGE, ST. BOTOLPH. The East Anglian, ii. 58.
   „   ST. ANDREW THE GREAT. The East Anglian, ii. 58.
   „   ST. MARY THE LESS. The East Anglian, ii. 11.
   „   ST. MARY THE GREAT. The East Anglian, ii. 110, 154.
Hare's Miscell. Par. Registers, MS. in Coll. Arms, 195.
   „   ALL SAINTS'. The East Anglian, ii. 110, 154.

CAMPSALL. Chester MSS. in Coll. Arms, (Yorkshire,) ii. 343.

CAMPTON-CUM-SHEFFORD. Blades' Genealogia Bedfordiensis, 60.

CAMPTON. Collectanea Topographica et Genealogica, iii. 121.

CANTERBURY, CATHEDRAL. Vol. II. of Publications of Harleian Society, Register Section, 1564-1878. Edited by Robert Hovenden.
   „   The Booke of Regester of St. Peter in Canterbury, 1560-1800. Edited by J. M. Cowper. Canterbury, 1888, 8vo.
   „   The Register Booke of St. Alphage in the Cyttye of Canterburye, 1558-1800. Edited by J. M. Cowper. Canterbury, 1889, 8vo.
   „   The Register Booke of St. Dunstan's, Canterbury, 1559-1800. Edited by J. M. Cowper. Canterbury, 1887, 8vo.
   „   The names of them that were Crystened, Marryed and Buryd in the Paryshe of St. Mary Magdalene in Canterbury, 1559-1800. Edited by J. M. Cowper. Canterbury, 1890, 8vo.
   „   ST. MILDRED. Chester MSS. in Coll. Arms, (Kent,) ii. 143.

CARBURTON. The Registers of Carburton, 1528-1812. Edited by George W. Marshall. Worksop, 1888, fol.

CARDINGTON. Blades' Genealogia Bedfordiensis, 63. Chester MSS. in Coll. Arms, (Bedfordshire,) 321, 369.

CAREBY, Chester MSS. in Coll. Arms, (Lincolnshire,) ii. 100.

CARHAMPTON. Chester MSS. in Coll. Arms, (Somerset,) i. 143.

CARLBY. Chester MSS. in Coll. Arms, (Lincolnshire,) i. 269, 395.

CARLTON. The Parish Registers of Carlton, Suffolk, 1538-1885. Privately printed for F. A. Crisp, 1886, fol.

CARLTON. Blades' Genealogia Bedfordiensis, 69. Harvey's Hundred of Willey, 259.

CARLTON-IN-LINDRICK.* Carlton-in-Lindrick Parish Magazine, July, 1886 — Dec. 1888.

CARLTON SCROOP. Chester MSS. in Coll. Arms, (Lincolnshire,) ii. 188.

CARSHALTON. Parish Registers, MS. in Coll. Arms, E. L. 11, fol. 1. Chester MSS. in Coll. Arms, (Surrey,) i. 357-393.

CARSINGTON. Chester MSS. in Coll. Arms, (Derbyshire,) i. 59.

* A MS. copy of this register, Marriages 1559-1754, and Baptisms and Burials 1559-1678, with extracts after to 1783, is in the library of Dr. Marshall, of the Heralds' College.

CARTMEL. Stockdale's Annals of Cartmel, 549. Chester MSS. in Coll. Arms, (Lancashire,) 375-390.

CASSINGTON. Chester MSS. in Coll. Arms, (Oxfordshire,) i. 297.

CASTLE BYTHAM. Chester MSS. in Coll. Arms, (Lincolnshire,) ii. 109.

CASTLE HEDINGHAM. The East Anglian, ii. 33.

CASTOR. Chester MSS. in Coll. Arms, (Northampton,) i. 237.

CATTISTOCK. Jewitt's Reliquary, xxvi. 137-144.

CAVERSHAM. Chester MSS. in Coll. Arms, (Oxfordshire,) i. 301.

CHADWELL. Chester MSS. in Coll. Arms. (Essex,) i. 15.

CHAGFORD. Chester MSS. in Coll. Arms, (Devon,) i. 27.

CHALGRAVE. Blades' Genealogia Bedfordiensis, 71. Chester MSS. in Coll. Arms, (Bedfordshire,) 371.

CHAPEL-EN-LE-FRITH. The Reliquary, vi. 66, 226. Chester MSS. in Coll. Arms, (Derbyshire,) i. 33.

CHARING. Chester MSS. in Coll. Arms, (Kent,) ii 97-112.

CHARLBURY. Chester MSS. in Coll. Arms, (Oxfordshire.) i. 305.

CHARLTON. Hasted's Kent, Hundred of Blackheath, by H. H. Drake, 142.

CHARLTON KINGS. Notes and Queries, 5 S. v. 82. Gloucestershire Notes and Queries, i. 31. Miscellanea Genealogica et Heraldica, New Series, ii. 301.

CHARTERHOUSE WITHAM. Chester MSS. in Coll. Arms, (Somerset,) i. 259.

CHASTLETON. Chester MSS. in Coll. Arms, (Oxfordshire,) i. 18-33.

CHATHAM. Chester MSS. in Coll. Arms, (Kent,) i. 15.

CHEADLE. Chester MSS. in Coll. Arms, (Cheshire,) 373.

CHELLINGTON. Blades' Genealogia Bedfordiensis, 74. Harvey's Hundred of Willey, 274.

CHELMSFORD. Chester MSS. in Coll. Arms, (Essex,) iii. 201.

CHELSTON. MS. in Coll. Arms, R. B. G. xxiii. 137.

CHELTENHAM. Gloucestershire Notes and Queries, i. 22, 228, 254, 295, 299, 308. Miscellanea Genealogica et Heraldica, New Series, iii. 32, 53, 70. MS. in Coll. Arms, J. P. cxcii. 419.

CHESTER, ST. BRIDGIT. Baptisms, 1560-1638; Marriages, 1560-1637; Burials, 1560-1666. British Museum, Harleian MS. 2177. In the handwriting of Randle Holme, and is a transcript of the Registers for the years mentioned. Some extracts from it are printed in Cheshire Notes and Queries, New Series, ii. 62-65.

„ ST. MARY-ON-THE-HILL. Baptisms, 1547-1572; Marriages, 1547-1551; Burials, 1547-1553. Harleian MS. 2177.

„ ST. OLAVE. Baptisms, Marriages, and Burials, 1611-1644, and Burials, 1654-1673. Harleian MS. 2177.

„ TRINITY. 1598-1653. Harleian MS. 2177.

„ ST. PETER. Chester MSS. in Coll. Arms, (Cheshire,) 287.

„ ST. JOHN. Chester MSS. in Coll. Arms, (Cheshire,) 289.

CHESTERFIELD. The Reliquary, viii. 9-19. Chester MSS. in Coll. Arms, (Derbyshire,) i. 141-162; ii. 1-182.

CHESTER-LE-STREET. Chronicon Mirabile, or Extracts from Parish Registers, 29. MS. in Coll. Arms, J. P. cxcv. 35.

CHESTERTON. Hare's Miscell. Par. Registers, MS. in Coll. Arms, 231.
CHEVELEY. Hare's Miscell. Par. Registers, MS. in Coll. Arms, 177.
CHICHELEY. Chester MSS. in Coll. Arms, (Bucks,) 131.
CHIDDINGFOLD. Chester MSS. in Coll. Arms, (Surrey,) iv. 257.
CHIGWELL. Chester MSS. in Coll. Arms, (Essex,) ii. 99-106.
CHILDSWICKHAM. Excerpta ex Registris Parochialibus in Com. Gloucester. Middle Hill, 1854, fol.
CHILDWALL. Original (Bishops') transcripts, 1670. British Museum, Add. MS. 32344.
CHILLESFORD. The Parish Registers of Chillesford. Privately printed for F. A. Crisp, 1886, fol.
CHIPPENHAM. Chester MSS. in Coll. Arms, (Wilts,) 89.
CHIPPING CAMPDEN. Chester MSS. in Coll. Arms, (Gloucestershire,) 127.
CHIPPING NORTON. Extracts from Chipping Norton Registers. Privately printed by Sir T. Phillipps, 4 pp. fol.
CHIPSTEAD. Chester MSS. in Coll. Arms, (Surrey,) iv. 279.
CHOLMWORTH. Blades' Genealogia Bedfordiensis, 82.
CHRISTON. Chester MSS. in Coll. Arms, (Somerset,) i. 317-338.
CHURCHAM. MS. in Coll. Arms, R. B. G. xxxviii. 28.
CHURCH MINSHULL. Chester MSS. in Coll. Arms, (Cheshire,) 161.
CHUTE. Collectanea Topographica et Genealogica, viii. 190.
CLAPHAM. Blades' Genealogia Bedfordiensis, 75.
CLAPHAM. Chester MSS. in Coll. Arms, (Surrey,) i. 1-188.
CLAPTON-IN-GORDANO. Chester MSS. in Coll. Arms, (Somerset,) i. 35.
CLAVERLEY. Original (Bishops') transcripts, 1636-1812. British Museum, Add. MS. 28739.
CLAXBY. Chester MSS. in Coll. Arms, (Lincolnshire,) iv. 119.
CLAXBY-BY-NORMANBY. Chester MSS. in Coll. Arms, (Lincolnshire,) ii. 354.
CLAYDON. Chester MSS. in Coll. Arms, (Oxfordshire,) ii. 319.
CLEE. Chester MSS. in Coll. Arms, (Lincolnshire,) iii. 392 ; iv. 155.
CLENT. Chester MSS. in Coll. Arms, (Worcestershire,) 85.
CLEWER. Chester MSS. in Coll. Arms, (Berkshire,) 12.
CLIFTON. Blades' Genealogia Bedfordiensis, 77.
CLOFORD. Chester MSS. in Coll. Arms, (Somerset,) i. 147.
CLOPHILL. Blades' Genealogia Bedfordiensis, 79.
CLYST, ST. MARY. MS. in Coll. Arms, J. P. cxcii. 266.
COATES. Chester MSS. in Coll. Arms, (Lincolnshire,) i. 38.
COATES, GREAT. Chester MSS. in Coll. Arms, (Lincolnshire,) iv. 31.
COATES, LITTLE. Chester MSS. in Coll. Arms, (Lincolnshire,) iv. 117.
COATES, NORTH. Chester MSS. in Coll. Arms, (Lincolnshire,) iv. 33.
COCKAYNE HATLEY. Blades' Genealogia Bedfordiensis, 81.
COLCHESTER. Registers of St. Leonard's, Colchester, 1670-71. Printed by F. A. Crisp, 1885, fol.
COLD ASHTON. MS. in Coll. Arms, R. B. G. xxxviii. 27.
COLD NORTON. Chester MSS. in Coll. Arms, (Essex,) i. 243.
COLEBY. Chester MSS. in Coll. Arms, (Lincolnshire,) i. 19
COLEY. See NORTHOWRAM.

COLESHILL. Chester MSS. in Coll. Arms, (Berkshire,) 141.
COLLINGBOURNE DUCIS. Collectanea Topographica et Genealogica, vii. 72.
COLLINGBOURNE KINGSTON. Collectanea Topographica et Genealogica, viii. 175.
COLLYWESTON. The Genealogist, ii. 151, 266, 394 ; iv. 166.
COLMER. See PRIORS' DEAN.
COLN ST. ALDWYN. MS. in Coll. Arms, R. B. G. xxxviii. 17.
COLSTERWORTH. Chester MSS. in Coll. Arms, (Lincolnshire,) ii. 367 ; v. 349.
COMPTON BASSETT. Chester MSS. in Coll. Arms, (Wilts.) 13.
COMPTON MARTIN. Chester MSS. in Coll. Arms, (Somerset,) i. 153.
COMPTON PAUNCEFOOT. Chester MSS. in Coll. Arms, (Somerset,) ii. 15.
CONGRESBURY. Chester MSS. in Coll. Arms, (Somerset,) ii. 21.
CONISBOROUGH. British Museum, Add. MS. 24439.
CONISHOLM. Chester MSS. in Coll. Arms, (Lincolnshire,) i. 127.
CONSCLIFFE. Chronicon Mirabile, or Extracts from Parish Registers, 65.
COPLE. Collectanea Topographica et Genealogica, v. 362. Blades' Genealogia Bedfordiensis, 84.
CORBY. Chester MSS. in Coll. Arms, (Lincolnshire.) ii. 104.
CORK. The Registers of the Parish of the Holy Trinity (Christ Church), Cork, from July, 1643, to February, 1668. Edited by Richard Caulfield. Cork, 1887, 8vo.
CORK. Baptist Register at Cork. Notes and Queries, 6 S. iii. 41, 121.
CORNWOOD. The Genealogist, vii. 164.
CORRINGHAM. Chester MSS. in Coll. Arms, (Lincolnshire,) i. 59.
CORSTON. Chester MSS. in Coll. Arms, (Somerset,) iii. 163.
CORTON DENHAM. Chester MSS. in Coll. Arms, (Somerset,) i. 289.
COTGRAVE. Chester MSS. in Coll. Arms, (Notts,) ii. 104.
COTTINGHAM. MS. in Coll. Arms, R. B. G. xxiii. 128.
COTTISFORD. Chester MSS. in Coll. Arms, (Oxfordshire,) i. 317.
COUGHTON. Chester MSS. in Coll. Arms, (Warwickshire,) 105.
COWFOLD. Chester MSS. in Coll. Arms, (Sussex,) i. 315.
COWLEY. Chester MSS. in Coll. Arms, (Oxfordshire,) iii. 397.
COVENHAM, ST. MARY. Chester MSS. in Coll. Arms, (Lincolnshire,) i. 174.
,, ST. BARTHOLOMEW. Chester MSS. in Coll. Arms, (Lincolnshire,) i. 175.
CRANESLEY. MS. in Coll. Arms, R. B. G. xxiii. 128.
CRANLEY. Chester MSS. in Coll. Arms, (Surrey,) iv. 253.
CRANFIELD. Blades' Genealogia Bedfordiensis, 87.
CRAWLEY. Chester MSS. in Coll. Arms, (Sussex,) ii. 37-54.
CRAYFORD. Chester MSS. in Coll. Arms, (Kent,) ii. 163.
CREETING, ST. PETER. Chester MSS. in Coll. Arms, (Suffolk,) 11.
CRICCIETH. The Genealogist, vii. 156.
CROFT. Chronicon Mirabile, or Extracts from Parish Registers, 149.
,, Chester MSS. in Coll. Arms, (Lincolnshire,) i. 79.

CRONDALL. Chester MSS. in Coll. Arms, (Hants,) 291.

CROPREDY. Chester MSS. in Coll. Arms, (Oxfordshire,) iii. 185.

CROWHURST. Chester MSS. in Coll. Arms, (Surrey,) iv. 389.

CROWLE. Chester MSS. in Coll. Arms, (Lincolnshire,) v. 231.

CROWMARSH GIFFORD. Chester MSS. in Coll. Arms, (Oxfordshire,) ii. 349.

CROYDON. Collectanea Topographica et Genealogica, ii. 292; iii. 307 ; iv. 91 ; v. 42. Steinman's History of Croydon, xix.-xxiv., 152-156. Chester MSS. in Coll. Arms, (Surrey,) iv. 291-372. MS. in Coll. Arms, J. P. clxxxix. 29.

CROYLAND. Chester MSS. in Coll. Arms, (Lincolnshire,) i. 102 ; v. 287.

CROXALL. The Register of Croxall Parish, 1586-1812 ; in 'An Historical Sketch of Croxall,' by Richard Ussher, pp. 83-119.

CULPHO. The Parish Registers of Culpho, 1721-1886. Privately printed for F. A. Crisp, 1886, fol.

CUMBERWORTH. Chester MSS. in Coll. Arms, (Lincolnshire,) i. 352.

CURRY RIVELL. Chester MSS. in Coll. Arms, (Somerset,) iii. 131.

DAGENHAM. Notes and Queries, 3 S. ii. 382. Chester MSS. in Coll. Arms, (Essex,) i. 263-306.

DARESBURY. Chester MSS. in Coll. Arms, (Cheshire,) 1-74.

DATCHET. Chester MSS. in Coll Arms, (Bucks,) 20.

DAVINGTON. Alphabetical Index to the Registers of Davington, co. Kent, 1549-1862. British Museum, Add. MS. 28837.

DEANE. Blades' Genealogia Bedfordiensis, 89.

„ Chester MSS. in Coll. Arms, (Lancashire,) 223.

DEBDEN. Chester MSS. in Coll. Arms, (Essex). A complete transcript, 1557-1777, ii. 323 ; iii. 1-118. The East Anglian, ii. 53 ; iii. 70, 337.

DEDHAM. Chester MSS. in Coll. Arms, (Essex,) i. 368-403.

DEEPING, ST. JAMES. Chester MSS. in Coll. Arms, (Lincolnshire,) i. 378.

DEMBLEBY. Chester MSS. in Coll. Arms, (Lincolnshire,) ii. 146.

DENCHWORTH. Chester MSS. in Coll. Arms, (Berkshire,) 131.

DENHAM. Hare's Miscell. Par. Registers, MS. in Coll. Arms, 235.

DENTON. The First Register Book of Baptisms, Marriages, and Burials solemnized at the Chapel of Denton, in the Parish of Gainford, and County of Durham. Transcribed by John Richard Walbran. 1586-1662. Ripon, 1842, 8vo. Only eight copies printed. The Antiquities of Gainford, by J. R. Walbran, 122. Chronicon Mirabile, or Extracts from Parish Registers, 63.

DEPTFORD. Hasted's Kent, Hundred of Blackheath, by H. H. Drake, 37.

DERBY, ST. ALKMUND. The Reliquary, x. 193 ; xi. 109, 135 ; xii. 9. Chester MSS. in Coll. Arms, (Derbyshire,) i. 121.

„ ALL SAINTS'. Chester MSS. in Coll. Arms, (Derbyshire,) i. 115.

„ ST. MICHAEL. Chester MSS. in Coll. Arms, (Derbyshire,) i. 111.

DERBY, ST. PETER. Chester MSS. in Coll. Arms, (Derbyshire,) i. 103.
  „ ST. WERBERGH. Chester MSS. in Coll. Arms, (Derbyshire,) i. 113.
DEWSBURY. Chester MSS. in Coll. Arms, (Yorkshire,) i. 365.
DICKLEBURGH. The East Anglian, iv. 181.
DIDCOT. Berkshire Notes and Queries, i. 63.   (In progress.)
DIDMARTON. MS. in Coll. Arms, R. B. G. xxxviii. 22.
DIGSWELL. Chester MSS. in Coll. Arms, (Herts,) ii. 127.
DINGLEY. MS. in Coll. Arms, R. B. G. xxiii. 104.
DINSDALE. Chronicon Mirabile, or Extracts from Parish Registers, 38.
DISLEY. Chester MSS. in Coll Arms, (Cheshire,) 329.
DITCHEAT. Chester MSS. in Coll. Arms, (Somerset,) iii. 53.
DODINGTON. Chester MSS. in Coll. Arms, (Kent.) i. 127-150.
  „ (co. Gloucester). Gloucestershire Notes and Queries, ii. 433.
DONCASTER. Jackson's History of St. George's Church, Doncaster, App. xxix-l.   Historical Notices of Doncaster, by C. W. Hatfield, 1 Series, 358-472 ; 2 Series, 29, 39, 60, 74, 79, 184, 187, 482, 486 ; 3 Series, 21, 91, 106-122, 126, 171, 188, 203, 270, 296, 327-381.   British Museum, Add. MSS. 24439, 24469, 24578.
DONCASTER. Marriages at Friends' Meeting-house, 1794-1865.   Historical Notices of Doncaster, by C. W. Hatfield, 2 Series, 368.
DONINGTON. Chester MSS. in Coll. Arms, (Lincolnshire,) ii. 93.
DOVER, ST. JAMES. Chester MSS. in Coll. Arms, (Kent,) i. 123.
  „ Registers of the French Church at Dover.   Privately printed by F. A. Crisp, 1888, fol.
DOWDESWELL. Chester MSS. in Coll. Arms, (Gloucestershire,) 305.
DOWLES. J. R. Burton's History of Bewdley, App. xliii.
DOWN. Nichols' Topographer, ii. 280, 532.   MS. in Coll. Arms, R. B. G. xxxviii. 1.
DOWNTON. Chester MSS. in Coll. Arms, (Wilts,) 41-87.
DOWSBY. Chester MSS. in Coll. Arms, (Lincolnshire,) ii. 153.
DOYNTON. Gloucestershire Notes and Queries, ii. 435.
DRIBY. Chester MSS. in Coll. Arms, (Lincolnshire,) i. 246.
DRIFFIELD. MS. in Coll. Arms, R. B. G. xxxviii. 26.
DRONFIELD. British Museum, Add. MS. 24570.   Chester MSS. in Coll. Arms, (Derbyshire,) i. 45, 277.
DRYPOOL. The Reliquary, x. 54 ; xi. 88.
DUBLIN, ST. AUDOENS. The Irish Builder, Vol. xxix.
  „ ST. NICHOLAS. Nichols' Topographer, ii. 520.
DUCKINFIELD. Extracts from the Registers of the Nonconformist Chapel at Duckinfield, co. Chester.   By J. P. Earwaker.   Liverpool, 1882, 8vo.   Reprint from Transactions of the Historic Society of Lancashire and Cheshire.
DUCKLINGTON. An Index to the Registers of Baptisms, Marriages, and Burials in the Parish of Ducklington.   By the Rev. W. D. Macray.   1550-1880.   Oxford, 1881, 8vo.   In transactions of the North Oxfordshire Archaeological Society for the year 1880.
DUDDINGTON. Chester MSS. in Coll. Arms, (Northampton,) i. 89.
DUFFIELD. The Reliquary, xxiii. 104, 134.

DUMMER. Chester MSS. in Coll. Arms, (Hants.) 217-227.
DUNHOLM Chester MSS. in Coll. Arms, (Lincolnshire,) ii. 3.
DUNKSBOURNE MILITIS. MS. in Coll. Arms, R. B. G. xxxviii. 25.
DUNSBY. Chester MSS. in Coll. Arms, (Lincolnshire,) i. 324.
DUNSTABLE. Blades' Genealogia Bedfordiensis, 92.
DUNSTER. Chester MSS. in Coll. Arms, (Somerset,) i. 157.
DUNS TEW. Chester MSS. in Coll. Arms, (Oxfordshire,) ii. 359.
DUNTON. Blades' Genealogia Bedfordiensis, 95.
DURHAM, ST. GILES. Chronicon Mirabile, or Extracts from Parish Registers, 56.
„ ST. MARGARET. Chronicon Mirabile, or Extracts from Parish Registers, 51.
„ ST. MARY-LE-BOW. Chronicon Mirabile, or Extracts from Parish Registers, 53.
„ ST. MARY NORTH BAYLEY. Chronicon Mirabile, or Extracts from Parish Registers, 53.
„ ST. NICHOLAS. Chronicon Mirabile, or Extracts from Parish Registers, 47.
„ ST. OSWALD. Chronicon Mirabile, or Extracts from Parish Registers, 41.
„ CATHEDRAL. Chronicon Mirabile, or Extracts from Parish Registers, 30.
DURLEY. Chester MSS. in Coll. Arms, (Hants,) 229.
DURNFORD. Parish Register of Durneford, Wilts, 1574-1650. Printed by Sir Thomas Phillipps, circa 1823, 8vo. pp. 50.
DYRHAM. Gloucestershire Notes and Queries, ii. 536, 592.

EAGLE. Chester MSS. in Coll. Arms, (Lincolnshire,) ii. 205.
EASINGTON. Chronicon Mirabile, or Extracts from Parish Registers, 15.
EAST ANTONY. Heraldic Church Notes from Cornwall, by. A. J. Jewers, 54.
EAST BARNET. Chester MSS, in Coll. Arms, (Herts,) ii. 191.
EAST BRIDGFORD. Chester MSS. in Coll. Arms, (Notts,) ii. 86.
EAST DEREHAM. Chester MSS, in Coll. Arms, (Norfolk,) ii. 51-148.
EAST HADDON. Chester MSS. in Coll. Arms, (Northampton), i. 47-68.
EAST HALTON. Chester MSS. in Coll. Arms, (Lincolnshire,) iv. 35.
EAST HAM. Chester MSS. in Coll. Arms, (Essex,) i. 233.
EASTHAM (co. Worcester). The Genealogist, iii. 133. The Reliquary, xviii. 208 ; xxiii. 220 ; xxiv. 45.
EAST LEACH TURVILLE. MS. in Coll. Arms, R. B. G. xxxviii. 19.
EAST LULWORTH. Chester MSS. in Coll. Arms, (Dorset,) 193.
EAST MARKHAM. Chester MSS. in Coll. Arms. (Notts,) ii. 91.
EASTON (Wilts). Collectanea Topographica et Genealogica, v. 39.
EASTON. Chester MSS. in Coll. Arms, (Northampton,) i. 385.
EASTON-IN-GORDANO. Chester MSS. in Coll. Arms, (Somerset,) iii. 167.
EAST RETFORD. The Reliquary, xvi. 217 ; xvii. 41, 109. Chester MSS. in Coll. Arms, (Notts,) ii. 1-17.

EAST TISTED. Chester MSS. in Coll. Arms, (Hants,) 237.

EAST TUDDENHAM. Chester MSS. in Coll. Arms, (Norfolk,) i. 395.

EATON BRAY. Blades' Genealogia Bedfordiensis, 97.

EATON SOCON. Blades' Genealogia Bedfordiensis, 100.

EBBERSTON. The Registers of Ebberston and Allerston, co. York. Ebberston and Allerston Parish Magazine, commencing with the No. for June, 1887, 4to.

EBRINGTON. Chester MSS. in Coll. Arms, (Gloucestershire,) 7. MS. in Coll. Arms, R. B. G. xxxviii. 14.

ECCLESFIELD. The First Book of the Registers of Ecclesfield Parish Church. Annotated by Alfred Scott Gatty. London, 1878. 4to. Baptisms, 1599 - 1619 ; Marriages, 1558 - 1621 ; Burials, 1558-1603.

ECKINGTON. British Museum, Add. MS. 24572.

EDBURTON. Copy of Parish Register Book, 1558-1673. By Rev. C. H. Wilkie. Brighton, 1884, 8vo. Index to same, privately printed by F. A. Crisp, 1887, 8vo.

EDENHAM. Chester MSS. in Coll. Arms, (Lincolnshire,) ii. 55.

EDITH WESTON. The Genealogist, i. 292, 334, 362.

EDMONTON. William Robinson's History of Edmonton, 68-73.

EDWORTH. Blades' Genealogia Bedfordiensis, 104.

EGTON. Chester MSS. in Coll. Arms, (Yorkshire,) i. 199-342. The entire Register. Marriages, 1622-1761 ; Baptisms and Burials, 1622-1779.

ELLOUGH. The Parish Registers of Ellough, Suffolk. 1540-1812. Privately printed for F. A. Crisp. London, 1886, 8vo.

ELSTEAD. Chester MSS. in Coll. Arms, (Surrey,) iv. 281.

ELSTOW. Blades' Genealogia Bedfordiensis, 105.

ELTHAM. Hasted's Kent, Hundred of Blackheath, by H. H. Drake, 210. MS. in Coll. Arms, R. B. G. xxiii. 146.

ELTON. Chronicon Mirabile, or Extracts from Parish Registers, 34.

ELY, ST. MARY'S. Chester MSS. in Coll. Arms, (Cambridgeshire,) 45-64.

" „ HOLY TRINITY. Chester MSS. in Coll. Arms, (Cambridgeshire,) 65-127.

ENFIELD (co. Middx.). Robinson's History of Enfield, ii. 89-103.

ENSTONE. Chester MSS. in Coll. Arms, (Oxfordshire,) iii. 365.

EPPING. Chester MSS. in Coll. Arms, (Essex,) ii. 139-301.

ERITH. Extracts from the Registers of the Parish Church of Erith. London, 1879, fol. Edited by R. Hovenden.

ERWARTON. MS. in Coll. Arms, J. P. cxciii. 25.

ERYHOLME. Chronicon Mirabile, or Extracts from Parish Registers, 124.

ETON. MS. in Coll. Arms, R. B. G. xxvii. 60.

EVEDON. Chester MSS. in Coll. Arms, (Lincolnshire,) ii. 81.

EVERSHOLT. Blades' Genealogia Bedfordiensis, 108.

EVESHAM, ST. LAWRENCE. Chester MSS. in Coll. Arms, (Worcestershire,) 197.

EVESHAM, ALL SAINTS. Chester MSS. in Coll. Arms, (Worcester-shire,) 201.
EWHURST. MS. in Coll. Arms, J. P. cxcv. 69.
EXETER, ST. MARTIN. Holwell's Devon, Coll. Arms, MS. J. P. xl. 16 23.
„ ST. MARY ARCHES. Holwell's Devon, Coll. Arms, MS., J. P. xl. 49-63.
„ ST. MARY-THE-MORE. Holwell's Devon, Coll. Arms, MS. J.P. xl. 79-90.
„ ST. OLAVE. Holwell's Devon, Coll. Arms, MS. J. P., xl. 64-70.
„ ST. SYDWELL. Holwell's Devon, Coll. Arms, MS. J. P. xl. 35-58. Coll. Arms, MS. R. B. G. xxix. Coll. Arms, MS. J. P. 192, 41.
„ ST. PETROCK. Chester MSS. in Coll. Arms, (Devon,) i. 285. ·
EXHALL-WITH-WIXFORD. The Genealogist, i. 128, 131.
EXMINSTER. Coll. Arms, MS. J. P. cxcii. 343.
EXMOUTH. See LITTLEHAM.
EYAM. Chester MSS. in Coll. Arms, (Derbyshire,) i. 35.
EYWORTH. Blades' Genealogia Bedfordiensis, 110.

FALDINGWORTH. Chester MSS. in Coll. Arms, (Lincolnshire,) i. 24.
FALKINGHAM. Chester MSS. in Coll. Arms, (Lincolnshire,) i. 360 ; v. 299.
FAREHAM. Chester MSS. in Coll. Arms, (Hants,) 131-148.
FARNDISH. Blades' Genealogia Bedfordiensis, 111. Harvey's Hundred of Willey, 419.
FARNDON. Collectanea Topographica et Genealogica, iv. 233.
FAULKBOURN. Chester MSS. in Coll. Arms, (Essex,) i. 18.
FAVERSHAM. Original (Bishops') Transcripts, 1730-1. British Museum, Add. MS. 32344.
FELMERSHAM Harvey's Hundred of Willey, 296. Blades' Genealogia Bedfordiensis, 112.
FELPHAM. Chester MSS. in Coll. Arms, (Sussex,) i. 366.
FEN DITTON. Hare's Miscell. Par. Registers, MS. in Coll. Arms, 188.
FENNY BENTLEY. The Reliquary, vii. 104.
FENTON-NEAR-NEWARK. Chester MSS. in Coll. Arms, (Lincolnshire,) ii. 1.
FETCHAM. MS. in Coll. Arms, J. P. cxciii. 360.
FEWSTON. Chester MSS. in Coll. Arms, (Yorkshire,) ii. 177.
FISKERTON. Chester MSS. in Coll. Arms, (Lincolnshire,) ii. 228, 317, 386, 400 ; iv. 61.
FISHLAKE. British Museum, Add. MS. 24469.
FLADBURY. Chester MSS. in Coll. Arms, (Worcestershire,) 81.
FLAMBOROUGH. Chronicon Mirabile, or Extracts from Parish Registers, 125.
FLAMSTED. Church Notes and Registers, MS. in Coll. Arms, 14.
FLEET. Chester MSS. in Coll. Arms, (Lincolnshire,) ii. 115, 267 ; v. 315.
FLINT. Historic Notices of Flint, by Henry Taylor, 160.

2

FLITTON. Blades' Genealogia Bedfordiensis, 116.
FLITWICK. Blades' Genealogia Bedfordiensis, 119.
FLIXTON. Chester MSS. in Coll. Arms, (Lancashire,) 195.
FO KE. Chester MSS. in Coll. Arms, (Dorset,) 1-12, 173.
FORCETT. Chronicon Mirabile, or Extracts from Parish Registers, 128.
FOREST HILL. Chester MSS. in Coll. Arms, (Oxfordshire,) i. 333.
FORNHAM, ALL SAINTS. Chester MSS. in Coll. Arms, (Suffolk,) 387.
FORTON. Chester MSS. in Coll. Arms, (Staffordshire,) 17.
FOTHERBY. Chester MSS. in Coll. Arms, (Lincolnshire,) i. 167.
FRAMLINGHAM. Chester MSS. in Coll. Arms, (Suffolk,) 261.
FRAMPTON COTTRELL. MS. in Coll. Arms, R. B. G. xxxviii. 24.
FRAMPTON-ON-SEVERN. Parish Registers, Glouc., MS. in Coll. Arms, R. B. G. xxii. 152.
FRANT. Chester MSS. in Coll. Arms, (Sussex,) i. 381.
FREMINGTON. Chester MSS. in Coll. Arms, (Devon,) iv. 217-264.
FRIESTHORP. Chester MSS. in Coll. Arms, (Lincolnshire,) v. 199.
FRITHELSTOCK. Chester MSS. in Coll. Arms, (Devon,) ii. 1-60.
FROME. Chester MSS. in Coll. Arms, (Somerset,) ii. 47 ; iii. 39.
FROSTENDEN. The Parish Registers of Frostenden, 1538-1791. Privately printed for F. A. Crisp. 1887, fol.
FROXFIELD. Collectanea Topographica et Genealogica, v. 36.
FULSTOW. Chester MSS. in Coll. Arms, (Lincolnshire,) iv. 163.
FYFIELD. Chester MSS. in Coll. Arms, (Berkshire,) 17.

GAINFORD. Index to the first vol. of the Parish Registers of Gainford. London, 1889, 8vo. Part i. contains Baptisms, 1560-1784 ; Part ii., Marriages, 1569-1761 ; Part iii., Burials, 1569-1784. The Antiquities of Gainford, by J. R. Walbran, 48. Chronicon Mirabile, or Extracts from Parish Registers, 69.
GAINSBOROUGH. Chester MSS. in Coll. Arms, (Lincolnshire,) iii. 159.
GARSINGTON. Chester MSS. in Coll. Arms, (Oxfordshire,) iii. 101
GARVESTON. Complete copy. 1539-1812. Chester MSS. in Coll. Arms, (Norfolk,) i. 255-354.
GATESHEAD. Chronicon Mirabile, or Extracts from Parish Registers, 26.
GEDNEY. Chester MSS. in Coll. Arms, (Lincolnshire,) ii. 96, 99, 268 ; v. 313.
GEDNEY HILL Chester MSS. in Coll. Arms, (Lincolnshire,) ii. 95 ; v. 311.
GENEVA (SWITZERLAND). 'Livre des Anglois,' Burn's History of Parish Registers, 2nd edition, App., 271-288.
GILLINGHAM. Chester MSS. in Coll. Arms, (Dorset,) 269.
GITTISHAM. Chester MSS. in Coll. Arms, (Devon,) i. 147.
GLANVILLE WOOTTON. Chester MSS. in Coll. Arms, (Dorset,) 21.
GLASTON. The Reliquary, xxv. 43, 91, 154, 217.
GLASTONBURY, ST. JOHN. Chester MSS. in Coll. Arms, (Somerset,) i. 291.

GLENTWORTH. Chester MSS. in Coll. Arms, (Lincolnshire,) i. 392.
GLOUCESTER, CATHEDRAL. Parish Registers, Glouc. MS. in Coll. Arms, R. B. G. xxii. 1.
,, ST. JOHN. Gloucestershire Notes and Queries, ii. 393. Parish Registers, Glouc., MS. in Coll. Arms, R. B. G. xxii. 29.
,, ST. MARY-DE-CRIPT. Parish Registers, Glouc. MS. in Coll. Arms, R. B. G. xxii. 72.
,, ST. MARY-DE-LOAD. Parish Registers, Glouc. MS. in Coll. Arms, R. B. G. xxii. 44.
,, ST. MICHAEL. Parish Registers, Glouc. MS. in Coll. Arms, R. B. G. xxii. 20.
,, ST. NICHOLAS. Parish Registers, Glouc. MS. in Coll. Arms, R. B. G. xxii. 63.
GOATHURST. The Genealogist, New Series, ii. 50, 96. Chester MSS. in Coll. Arms, (Somerset,) i. 179.
GODALMING. Chester MSS. in Coll. Arms, (Surrey,) iv. 271.
GOLDINGTON. Blades' Genealogia Bedfordiensis, 120.
GOLTHO. Chester MSS. in Coll. Arms, (Lincolnshire,) ii. 183.
GORING. Chester MSS. in Coll. Arms, (Sussex,) ii. 77.
GOSFIELD. Chester MSS. in Coll. Arms, (Essex,) ii. 29.
GOSPORT. Chester MSS. in Coll. Arms, (Hants,) 93-107.
GOXHILL. Chester MSS. in Coll. Arms, (Lincolnshire,) i. 105 ; v. 289.
GRAINSBY. Chester MSS. in Coll. Arms, (Lincolnshire,) i. 115 ; iv. 23.
GRANTHAM. Chester MSS. in Coll. Arms, (Lincolnshire,) iii. 114.
GRAPPENHALL. Chester MSS. in Coll. Arms, (Cheshire,) 89-130.
GRAVENHURST, UPPER. Blades' Genealogia Bedfordiensis, 126.
,, LOWER. Blades' Genealogia Bedfordiensis, 125.
GRAYINGHAM. Chester MSS. in Coll. Arms, (Lincolnshire,) i. 398.
GREAT AMWELL. Chester MSS. in Coll. Arms, (Herts,) ii, 1.
GREAT BILLING. Collectanea Topographica et Genealogica, viii. 189.
GREAT BOOKHAM. Chester MSS. in Coll. Arms, (Surrey,) iv. 259.
GREAT BRICKHILL. Chester MSS. in Coll. Arms, (Bucks,) 137.
GREAT BURSTEAD. Chester MSS. in Coll. Arms, (Essex,) i. 1.
GREAT CARLTON. Chester MSS. in Coll. Arms, (Lincolnshire,) ii. 20.
GREAT GADDESDEN. Chester MSS. in Coll. Arms, (Herts,) ii. 133. Church Notes and Registers, MS. in Coll. Arms, 15.
GREAT GRIMSBY. The Register Book of the Parish Church of St. James, Great Grimsby, 1538-1812. Edited by G. S. Stephenson, M.D. Great Grimsby, 1889, 8vo.
GREAT HALE. Chester MSS. in Coll. Arms, (Lincolnshire,) ii. 61.
GREATHAM. Chester MSS. in Coll. Arms, (Hants,) 167.
GREAT HAMPDEN. The Parish Registers of Great Hampden from 1557-1812. Edited by E. A. Ebblewhite. London, 1888, fol.
GREAT HORMEAD. Chester MSS. in Coll. Arms, (Herts,) ii. 121.
GREAT HORWOOD. Chester MSS. in Coll. Arms, (Bucks,) 145.
GREAT LIMBER. Chester MSS. in Coll. Arms, (Lincolnshire,) v. 21.
GREAT LINFORD. Chester MSS. in Coll. Arms, (Bucks,) 32.

GREAT LONGSDON. The Reliquary, ii. 155.
GREAT MARLOW. Chester MSS. in Coll. Arms, (Bucks,) 48.
GREAT MILTON. Chester MSS. in Coll. Arms, (Oxfordshire,) i. 137-156.
GREAT OUSEBURN. Chester MSS. in Coll. Arms, (Yorkshire,) ii. 171.
GREAT PARNDON. Chester MSS. in Coll. Arms, (Essex,) iii. 303-352.
GREAT PONTON. Chester MSS. in Coll. Arms, (Lincolnshire,) ii. 366.
GREAT ROLLRIGHT. Chester MSS. in Coll. Arms, (Oxfordshire,) iii. 17.
GREAT SAXHAM. Chester MSS. in Coll. Arms, (Suffolk,) 327.
GREAT TEW. Chester MSS. in Coll. Arms, (Oxfordshire,) iii. 51.
GREAT TORRINGTON. Chester MSS. in Coll. Arms, (Devon.) i. 23, 51.
GREAT WARLEY. Chester MSS. in Coll. Arms, (Essex,) i. 248.
GREENWICH. Hasted's Kent, Hundred of Blackheath, by H. H.
Drake, 113. Chester MSS. in Coll. Arms, (Kent,) i. 155-399.
MS. in Coll. Arms, J. P. clxxxviii. 124.
GREENWICH HOSPITAL. Chester MSS. in Coll. Arms, (Private
Chapels,) 357-373.
GREETWELL. Chester MSS. in Coll. Arms, (Lincolnshire.) ii. 221.
GRINDON. The Reliquary, v. 21.
GRINDON (co. Durham). MSS. in Coll. Arms, C. G. Y. clxxxvi. 159.

HABOROUGH. Chester MSS. in Coll. Arms, (Lincolnshire,) iv. 25.
HACKINGTON. Chester MSS. in Coll. Arms, (Kent,) ii. 135.
HADDENHAM. Chester MSS. in Coll. Arms, (Cambridgeshire.) 189.
HADDINGTON. (English Episcopal.) Northern Notes and Queries,
iii. 67, 118 ; iv. 39, 88, 127, 148.
HADLEIGH. Chester MSS. in Coll. Arms, (Suffolk,) 233.
    „   Chester MSS. in Coll. Arms, (Essex,) i. 4.
HAINTON. Chester MSS. in Coll. Arms, (Lincolnshire,) i. 286.
HALIFAX. Halifax Parish Church Registers, 1538-1541. Appendix
to 'Chapters on the early Registers of Halifax Parish Church.'
By W. J. Walker, Halifax, 1885, 4to. Chester MSS. in Coll.
Arms, (Yorkshire,) ii. 289.
HALTON. Chester MSS. in Coll. Arms, (Lancashire,) 1-120. Complete
transcript. Marriages, 1593-1754 ; Baptisms, 1592-1688 ; Burials,
1592-1795.
HAMPNETT. Marriages, 1737-1754. Gloucestershire Notes and
Queries, i. 240 ; ii. 550, 579.
HAMPSTHWAITE. Chester MSS. in Coll. Arms, (Yorkshire,) ii. 195.
HAMPTON LUCY. Chester MSS. in Coll. Arms, (Warwickshire,) 1.
HANBOROUGH. Chester MSS. in Coll. Arms, (Oxfordshire,) i. 355.
HANGLETON. Chester MSS. in Coll. Arms, (Sussex,) i. 287.
HANLEY-WILLIAM. The Genealogist, ii. 316.
HANSWORTH. British Museum, Add. MSS. 24439, 24570, 24568.
HARDINGHAM. Chester MSS. in Coll. Arms, (Norfolk,) i. 387.   MS.
in Coll. Arms, J. P. excvi. 3.
HARDWICK. Chester MSS. in Coll. Arms, (Norfolk,) i. 163.
HARDWICKE. Gloucestershire Notes and Queries, ii. 644.
HAREBY. Chester MSS. in Coll. Arms, (Lincolnshire,) i. 15.
HARGRAVE. MS. in Coll. Arms, R. B. G. xxiii. 138.

HARLINGTON. Blades' Genealogia Bedfordiensis, 127. Harvey's Hundred of Willey, 375.

HARMESTON. Chester MSS. in Coll. Arms, (Lincolnshire,) i. 21.

HARPENDEN. Chester MSS. in Coll. Arms, (Herts,) ii. 145. Church Notes and Registers, MS. in Coll. Arms, 16.

HARPSWELL. Chester MSS. in Coll. Arms, (Lincolnshire,) i. 57.

HARROLD. Harvey's Hundred of Willey, 340. Blades' Genealogia Bedfordiensis, 131.

HART. Chronicon Mirabile, or Extracts from Parish Registers, 7.

HARTLAND. Chester MSS. in Coll. Arms, (Devon,) iii. iv. Complete transcript. Marriages, 1557-1837 ; Baptisms, 1557-1812 ; Burials, 1557-1866.

HARTLEPOOL. Chronicon Mirabile, or Extracts from Parish Registers, 3.

HARTSHEAD. Chester MSS. in Coll. Arms, (Yorkshire,) ii. 267.

HARWELL. Chester MSS. in Coll. Arms, (Berkshire,) 67-78.

HASELBURY BRYAN. Chester MSS. in Coll. Arms, (Dorset,) 74.

HASTINGS, ST. CLEMENT. Parish Register, MS. in Coll. Arms, E. L. xii. 25.

HATFIELD. Chester MSS. in Coll. Arms, (Yorkshire,) ii. 305. British Museum, Add. MS. 24469.

HATHERSAGE. The Reliquary, x. 164, 239.

HATTON. Chester MSS. in Coll. Arms, (Lincolnshire,) ii. 144.

HAWERBY. Chester MSS. in Coll. Arms, (Lincolnshire,) iv. 41.

HAWKCHURCH. Chester MSS. in Coll. Arms, (Dorset,) 219.

HAWNES. Blades' Genealogia Bedfordiensis, 134. Collectanea Topographica et Genealogica, iii. 85. Chester MSS. in Coll. Arms, (Bedfordshire,) 337.

HAWORTH. Chester MSS. in Coll. Arms, (Yorkshire,) ii. 373.

HAWSTED. Cullum's History of Hawsted, 2nd edition, 73. Chester MSS. in Coll. Arms, (Suffolk,) 307.

HAXEY. Chester MSS. in Coll. Arms, (Lincolnshire,) ii. 291 ; v. 353.

HAYDOR. Chester MSS. in Coll. Arms, (Lincolnshire,) ii. 170 ; v. 323.

HAYS (co. Kent). Church Notes and Registers, MS. in Coll. Arms, 23.

HEADINGTON. Chester MSS. in Coll. Arms, (Oxfordshire,) iii. 83.

HEALING. Chester MSS. in Coll. Arms, (Lincolnshire,) iii. 405.

HEAPHAM. Chester MSS. in Coll. Arms, (Lincolnshire,) i. 384.

HECKINGTON. Chester MSS. in Coll. Arms, (Lincolnshire,) ii. 64-78.

HEDDON-ON-THE-WALL. Chronicon Mirabile, or Extracts from Parish Registers, 152.

HEDSOR. Church Notes and Registers, MS. in Coll. Arms, 6.

HEIGHINGTON. Chronicon Mirabile, or Extracts from Parish Registers, 35.

HELPRINGHAM. Chester MSS. in Coll. Arms, (Lincolnshire,) ii. 57.

HEMINGBOROUGH. Burton's History of Hemingborough. Edited by Canon Raine, 127-138.

HEMINGTON. Chester MSS. in Coll. Arms, (Somerset,) i. 117.

HEMPSTED. MS. in Coll. Arms, R. B. G. xxxviii. 6.

HEMSWELL. Chester MSS. in Coll. Arms, (Lincolnshire,) i. 387.

HENLOW. Blades' Genealogia Bedfordiensis, 136.

HENSTEAD. The East Anglian, iv. 107.

HESLEDEN. Chronicon Mirabile, or Extracts from Parish Registers, 10.

HEVENINGHAM. Hare's Miscell. Par. Registers, MS. in Coll. Arms, 159.

HEXHAM. Chronicon Mirabile, or Extracts from Parish Registers, 154.

HIGHCLERE. Nichols' Topographer, iii. 409.

HIGH ERCALL. Original (Bishops') transcripts, 1630, 1632-4, 1636, 1663-4. British Museum, Add. MS. 32344.

HIGHWORTH. Extracts from, privately printed by Sir T. Phillipps, pp. 8, no place or date, 8vo.

HILLESDEN. Chester MSS. in Coll. Arms, (Bucks,) 43.

HOCKLIFFE. Blades' Genealogia Bedfordiensis, 140.

HOE. Chester MSS. in Coll. Arms, (Norfolk,) ii. 1.

HOGSTHORPE. Chester MSS. in Coll. Arms, (Lincolnshire,) ii. 38.

HOLBEACH. Chester MSS. in Coll. Arms, (Lincolnshire,) i. 302.

HOLLACOMBE. A complete transcript, 1638-1738. Chester MSS. in Coll. Arms, (Devon,) ii. 383-392.

HOLNEST. Chester MSS. in Coll. Arms, (Dorset,) 29.

HOLTON. Chester MSS. in Coll. Arms, (Oxfordshire,) ii. 97; iii. 315.

HOLTON BECKERING. Chester MSS. in Coll. Arms, (Lincolnshire,) ii. 136.

HOLWELL. Blades' Genealogia Bedfordiensis, 142.

   ,,   Chester MSS. in Coll. Arms, (Dorset,) 73.

HOLY ISLAND. Chronicon Mirabile, or Extracts from Parish Registers, 107.

HONEYBORNE. Chester MSS. in Coll. Arms, (Worcestershire,) 187.

HOOTON PANNELL. British Museum, Add. MS. 24469.

   ,,   ROBERT. British Museum, Add. MS. 24469.

HORBLING. Chester MSS. in Coll. Arms, (Lincolnshire,) ii. 150.

HORBURY. Chester MSS. in Coll. Arms, (Yorkshire,) ii. 323.

HORLEY. Chester MSS. in Coll. Arms, (Oxfordshire,) i. 199.

HORNBY. Nichols' Topographer, iii. 325.

HORNCASTLE. Chester MSS. in Coll. Arms, (Lincolnshire,) iii. 205.

HORNCHURCH. Chester MSS. in Coll. Arms, (Essex,) i. 307-339; ii. 37-62. Notes and Queries, 3 S. ii. 245.

HORNINGSHEATH. Chester MSS. in Coll. Arms, (Suffolk,) 363.

HORNTON. Chester MSS. in Coll. Arms, (Oxfordshire,) i. 197.

HORSELL. Chester MSS. in Coll. Arms, (Surrey,) iv. 283.

HORSHAM. MS. in Coll. Arms, J. P. cxcii. 360

HORSINGTON. Chester MSS. in Coll. Arms, (Somerset,) i. 139.

HORSTED KEYNES. Miscellanea Genealogica et Heraldica, 2nd series, i. 193. Chester MSS. in Coll. Arms, (Sussex,) i. 25, 386; ii. 95.

HORTON. Gloucestershire Notes and Queries, iii. 3.

HOUGH-ON-THE-HILL. Chester MSS. in Coll. Arms, (Lincolnshire,) i. 329.

HOUGHTON CONQUEST. Blades' Genealogia Bedfordiensis, 143.

HOUGHTON REGIS. Blades' Genealogia Bedfordiensis, 152.
,, -LE-SPRING. Chronicon Mirabile, or Extracts from Parish Registers, 67.
HOVE. Chester MSS. in Coll. Arms, (Sussex,) i. 273.
HOWELL. Chester MSS. in Coll. Arms, (Lincolnshire,) ii. 79.
HULCOTE. Blades' Genealogia Bedfordiensis, 154.
HULL. A Register of Marriages in the Chappel of God's House Hospital, near Hull, since the first of May, 1695. Privately printed by Sir Thos. Phillipps, N.D. 3 pages, 12mo.
HULL, HOLY TRINITY. MS. in Coll. Arms, J. P. cxcv. 25.
HUNGERFORD. Collectanea Topographica et Genealogica, v. 359. Chester MSS. in Coll. Arms, (Berkshire,) 115.
HUNSDON. Chester MSS. in Coll. Arms, (Herts,) ii. 19, 171.
HUNTINGDON, ST. MARY. Chester MSS. in Coll. Arms, (Hunts,) 69.
HURSLEY. Chester MSS. in Coll. Arms, (Hants,) 315.
HURST. Chester MSS. in Coll. Arms, (Berkshire,) 121.
HURWORTH. Chronicon Mirabile, or Extracts from Parish Registers, 39.
HUSBORNE CRAWLEY. Blades' Genealogia Bedfordiensis, 155. Chester MSS. in Coll. Arms, (Bedfordshire,) 7.
HUTTOFT. Chester MSS. in Coll. Arms, (Lincolnshire,) iii. 376.
HUTTON. Chester MSS. in Coll. Arms, (Essex,) i. 245.

ICKLETON. The East Anglian, ii. 169.
IDYSLEIGH. The Genealogist, vii. 83.
IFIELD. Chester MSS. in Coll. Arms, (Sussex,) i. 325.
ILFRACOMBE. Chester MSS. in Coll. Arms, (Devon,) i. 1.
ILKLEY. Ilkley, Ancient and Modern, by R. Collyer and J. H Turner, 180.
IMMINGHAM. Chester MSS. in Coll. Arms, (Lincolnshire,) iv. 169.
INGLEBY GREENHOW. The Register Booke of Inglebye iuxta Greuhow, 1539-1800. By John Blackburne. Canterbury, 1889, 8vo.
IPSDEN. Chester MSS. in Coll. Arms, (Oxfordshire,) ii. 387.
IPSTONES. Chester MSS. in Coll. Arms, (Staffordshire,) 5.
IRBY-UPON-HUMBER. The Parish Register of Irby-upon-Humber, co. Lincoln, 1558-1785. Printed at the private press of F. A. Crisp, 1890, fol.
IRCHESTER. MS. in Coll. Arms, R. B. G. xxiii. 128.
IRNHAM. Chester MSS. in Coll. Arms, (Lincolnshire,) i. 322.
IRON ACTON. Gloucestershire Notes and Queries, iii. 51.
ISLEHAM. Chester MSS. in Coll. Arms, (Cambridgeshire,) 129-188.
ISLEWORTH. Aungier's History of Syon and Isleworth, 171-179.
ISLIP. Chester MSS. in Coll. Arms, (Oxfordshire,) i. 375.
IVER. Collectanea Topographica et Genealogica, iii. 279. Church Notes and Registers, MS. in Coll. Arms, 7.

JARROW. Chronicon Mirabile, or Extracts from Parish Registers, 6, 77.

KEDDINGTON. Chester MSS. in Coll. Arms, (Lincolnshire,) i. 227.

KEELBY. Chester MSS. in Coll. Arms, (Lincolnshire,) iv. 55.

KEGIDOG, *alias* St. George. The Parish Registers of Kegidog. *alias* St. George, 1694-1749. Printed at the private press of F. A. Crisp, 1890, fol.

KEIGHLEY. The Keighley Quaker Register. Yorkshire Notes and Queries, vol. ii., 87, 145, 225.

KELVEDON HATCH. Chester MSS. in Coll. Arms, (Essex,) i. 8.

KELSALE. The Parish Registers of Kelsale, Suffolk, 1538-1812. Printed for F. A. Crisp, 1887, fol.

KELSTERN. Chester MSS. in Coll. Arms, (Lincolnshire,) i. 292.

KEMPSFORD. The Registers of Kempsford. co. Gloucester, 1653-1700. Privately printed for F. A. Crisp, 1887, fol. MS. in Coll. Arms, R. B. G. xxxviii. 28.*

KEMPTON. Blades' Genealogia Bedfordiensis, 157-164.

KEMSING. The Genealogist, ii. 343. Chester MSS. in Coll. Arms, (Kent,) ii. 77.

KENCOTT. Chester MSS. in Coll. Arms, (Oxfordshire,) ii. 397.

KENN. Chester MSS. in Coll. Arms, (Somerset,) iii. 145.

KETTLETHORPE. Chester MSS. in Coll. Arms, (Lincolnshire,) i. 237.

KEYNSHAM. Chester MSS. in Coll. Arms, (Somerset,) i. 135.

KEYSOE. Blades' Genealogia Bedfordiensis, 165.

KILLINGHOLME. Chester MSS. in Coll. Arms, (Lincolnshire,) iv. 79.

KINGHAM. Chester MSS. in Coll. Arms, (Oxfordshire,) ii. 393.

KING'S CLERE. MS. in Coll. Arms, J. P. cxcv. 71.

KING'S CLIFFE. Chester MSS. in Coll. Arms, (Northampton,) i. 255.

KING'S LANGLEY. Chester MSS. in Coll. Arms, (Herts,) ii. 139.

KINGSNORTH. MS. in Coll. Arms, J. P. cxcv. 47.

KING'S SUTTON. Chester MSS. in Coll. Arms, (Northampton,) i. 69.

KINGSTON-NEAR-TAUNTON. Chester MSS. in Coll. Arms, (Somerset,) iii. 171.

KINGSTON-ON-THAMES. Chester MSS. in Coll. Arms, (Surrey,) ii. 153-216.

KINGSWINFORD. Chester MSS. in Coll. Arms, (Staffordshire,) 39.

KINTBURY. Chester MSS. in Coll. Arms, (Berkshire,) 103.

KIRKBURTON. The Parish Registers of Kirkburton, co. York. Edited by F. A. Collins. Vol. i., 1541-1654. Exeter, 1887, 8vo. The earlier portion of this register was printed in the Kirkburton Parish Magazine, 4to., pp. 164.

KIRBY FLEETHAM. Complete copy, 1591-1718. Chester MSS. in Coll. Arms, (Yorkshire,) i. 133-198.

KIRBY-ON-THE-MOOR. Chester MSS. in Coll. Arms, (Yorkshire,) ii. 173.

KIRKBY UNDERWOOD. Chester MSS. in Coll. Arms, (Lincolnshire,) ii. 120.

KIRKDALE. Complete copy, 1580-1762. Chester MSS. in Coll. Arms, (Yorkshire,) ii. 1-130.

KIRKBY-CUM-OSGODBY. Chester MSS. in Coll. Arms, (Lincolnshire,) v. 17.

* When Bigland made these notes the Register began in 1573.

KIRBY WHARF. British Museum, Add. MS. 24570.
KIRTLINGTON. Chester MSS. in Coll. Arms, (Oxfordshire,) i. 211.
KIRTON-IN HOLLAND. Chester MSS. in Coll. Arms, (Lincolnshire,) ii. 161, 371.
KIRTON-IN-LINDSEY. Chester MSS. in Coll. Arms, (Lincolnshire,) i. 61 ; iv. 69.
KNARESBOROUGH. Chester MSS. in Coll. Arms, (Yorkshire,) ii. 233.
KNEBWORTH. Apparently an original Register, on paper. Entries from 1596-1599, 1606-1650, 1663-1669, 1703-1719. MS. at Dr. Williams's Library, Grafton Street, W.C.
KNEESALL. Chester MSS. in Coll. Arms, (Notts,) ii. 48.
KNOTTING. Blades' Genealogia Bedfordiensis, 167.
KNOWLE (co. Dorset). MS. in Coll. Arms, J. P. cxcii. 270.
KYMPTON. Hare's Miscell. Par. Registers, MS. in Coll. Arms, 171.

LACEBY. Notes and Queries, 3 S. ii. 322. Chester MSS. in Coll. Arms, (Lincolnshire,) iv. 385.
LACKFORD. Chester MSS. in Coll. Arms, (Suffolk,) 393.
LAMBOURNE. The Parish Register of Lambourne, Essex, 1582-1709. Printed at the private press of F. A. Crisp, 1890, fol.
LAMESLEY. Chronicon Mirabile, or Extracts from Parish Registers, 36.
LANCAUT. MS. in Coll. Arms, R. B. G. xxxviii. 3.
LANCHESTER. Chronicon Mirabile, or Extracts from Parish Registers, 60.
LANGFORD. Blades' Genealogia Bedfordiensis, 168.
LANGFORD BUDVILLE. Chester MSS. in Coll. Arms, (Somerset,) i. 255.
LANGTON-BY-WRAGBY. Chester MSS. in Coll. Arms, (Lincolnshire,) ii. 186.
LATHBURY. Chester MSS. in Coll. Arms, (Bucks,) 34.
LAUGHTON. Chester MSS. in Coll. Arms, (Lincolnshire,) i. 63.
LAVENHAM. Chester MSS. in Coll. Arms, (Suffolk,) 219.
LAVINGTON, or LENTON. Chester MSS. in Coll. Arms, (Lincolnshire,) i. 4.
LAWFORD. Chester MSS. in Coll. Arms, (Essex,) i. 5.
LAXFIELD. The East Anglian, ii. 256. Chester MSS. in Coll. Arms, (Suffolk,) 71.
LAXTON. Chester MSS. in Coll. Arms, (Notts,) ii. 19-47.
LEA. Chester MSS. in Coll. Arms, (Lincolnshire,) i. 235.
LEADENHAM. Chester MSS. in Coll. Arms, (Lincolnshire,) i. 307.
LEAKE. Chester MSS. in Coll. Arms, (Lincolnshire,) ii. 201.
LEASINGHAM. Chester MSS. in Coll. Arms, (Lincolnshire,) ii. 19.
LECHLADE. MS. in Coll. Arms, R. B. G. xxxviii. 21, 33.
LECKHAMPSTEAD. Chester MSS. in Coll. Arms, (Bucks,) 65.
LEE. The Register of St. Margaret, Lee, from 1579-1754. Edited by L. L. Duncan and A. O. Barron. Lee, 1888, 8vo. Hasted's Kent, Hundred of Blackheath, by H. H. Drake, 234.
LEEK. The Reliquary, iii. 211. Chester MSS. in Coll. Arms, (Staffordshire.) i. 23.

LEEK WOTTON. Leek Wotton Register, co. Warwick, 1685-1742.
Printed by Sir Thos. Phillipps, pp. 9. N.D., 8vo. Index to Parish
Registers of Leek Wotton, 1685-1742. Privately printed by F. A.
Crisp, 1887, 8vo.
LEGSBY. Chester MSS. in Coll. Arms, (Lincolnshire,) ii. 131.
LEICESTER, ST. NICHOLAS. Leicestershire Architectural Society, vii.
31, 195.
LEIGH. The Register of the parish of Leigh, Lancashire, 1559-1624.
Edited by J. H. Stanning. Leigh, 1882, 8vo. Chester MSS. in
Coll. Arms, (Lancashire,) 231-373.
LEIGH. Chester MSS. in Coll. Arms, (Essex,) iii. 389.
LEIGHTON BUZZARD. Blades' Genealogia Bedfordiensis, 170 176.
Miscellanea Genealogica et Heraldica, new series, iii. 241, 258,
281, 295, 324. Chester MSS. in Coll. Arms, (Bedfordshire,) 94,
347-362.
LENHAM. Chester MSS. in Coll. Arms, (Kent,) ii. 113 131.
LENTON. Jewitt's Reliquary, xiii. 11. J. T. Godfrey's History of
Lenton, 274-285. Chester MSS. in Coll. Arms, (Notts,) ii. 64, 283.
LENTON. See LAVINGTON.
LEONARD STANLEY. Parish Registers Glouc., MS. in Coll. Arms,
R. B. G. xxii. 149, 158.
LEVELAND. Chester MSS. in Coll. Arms, (Kent,) ii. 148.
LEVERTON. Chester MSS. in Coll. Arms, (Lincolnshire,) ii. 202.
LEWKNOR. Chester MSS. in Coll. Arms, (Oxfordshire,) iii. 77.
LEWISHAM. Hasted's Kent, Hundred of Blackheath, by H. H. Drake,
275.
LICHFIELD, ST. MICHAEL. Chester MSS. in Coll. Arms, (Stafford-
shire,) 43.
    ,,   ST. CHAD. Chester MSS. in Coll. Arms, (Staffordshire,
49.
    ,,   ST. MARY. Chester MSS. in Coll. Arms, (Staffordshire,)
51.
    ,,   CATHEDRAL. Chester MSS. in Coll. Arms, (Staffordshire,)
57.
LIDLINGTON. Blades' Genealogia Bedfordiensis, 177.
LILFORD. Complete copy, 1564-1777. Chester MSS. in Coll. Arms,
(Northampton,) i. 175.
LILLINGSTONE LOVELL. Chester MSS. in Coll. Arms, (Oxfordshire,)
i. 381.
LIMPSFIELD. Chester MSS. in Coll. Arms, (Surrey,) iv. 263.
LINCOLN, ST. BENEDICT. Chester MSS. in Coll. Arms, (Lincolnshire,) iii. 39.
    ,,   ST. BOTOLPH. Chester MSS. in Coll. Arms, (Lincolnshire,)
iii. 34.
    ,,   ST. MARGARET-IN-THE-CLOSE. Chester MSS. in Coll.
Arms, (Lincolnshire,) iii. 75.
    ,,   ST. MARK. Chester MSS. in Coll. Arms, (Lincolnshire,)
iii. 9.
    ,,   ST. MARTIN. Chester MSS. in Coll. Arms, (Lincolnshire,)
iii. 1, 192.

LINCOLN, ST. MARY MAGDALEN. Chester MSS. in Coll. Arms, (Lincolnshire,) iii. 64, 195.
   „ ST. MARY-LE-WIGFORD. Chester MSS. in Coll. Arms, (Lincolnshire,) iii. 67.
   „ ST. MICHAEL-ON-THE-MOUNT. Chester MSS. in Coll. Arms, (Lincolnshire,) iii. 54.
   „ ST. NICHOLAS, NEWPORT. Chester MSS. in Coll. Arms, (Lincolnshire,) iii. 74.
   „ ST. PAUL-IN-THE-BAIL. Chester MSS. in Coll. Arms, (Lincolnshire,) iii. 7, 197.
   „ ST. PETER-AT-ARCHES. Chester MSS. in Coll. Arms, (Lincolnshire,) iii. 43, 190, 233.
   „ ST. PETER-IN-EASTGATE. Chester MSS. in Coll. Arms, (Lincolnshire,) iii. 59.
   „ ST. PETER-AT-GOWTS. Chester MSS. in Coll. Arms, (Lincolnshire,) iii. 15, 246.
   „ ST. SWITHIN. Chester MSS. in Coll. Arms, (Lincolnshire,) iii. 10.
LINDON. The Genealogist, iii. 329.
LINSTEAD. Chester MSS. in Coll. Arms, (Kent,) i. 151 ; ii. 157.
LINWOOD. Chester MSS. in Coll. Arms, (Lincolnshire,) v. 27.
LISSINGTON. Chester MSS. in Coll. Arms, (Lincolnshire,) v. 201.
LITTLE BARDFIELD. Chester MSS. in Coll. Arms, (Essex,) iii. 123.
LITTLE BURSTEAD. Chester MSS. in Coll. Arms, (Essex,) i. 17.
LITTLE CASTERTON. The Genealogist, i. 64, 154, 163.
LITTLE GRIMSBY. Chester MSS. in Coll. Arms, (Lincolnshire,) i. 74.
LITTLEHAM. Complete transcript, 1538-1812. Chester MSS. in Coll. Arms, (Devon,) v. 91-201.
LITTLEHAM-CUM-EXMOUTH. Chester MSS. in Coll. Arms, (Devon,) i. 273.
LITTLE ILFORD. Notes and Queries, 3 S. ii. 283 ; iii. 226. Chester MSS. in Coll. Arms, (Essex,) i. 354-367.
LITTLE MARLOW. Chester MSS. in Coll. Arms, (Bucks,) 55.
LITTLE PLUMSTEAD. The East Anglian, i. 305.
LITTLE SAXHAM. Chester MSS. in Coll. Arms, (Suffolk,) 323.
LITTLE TORRINGTON. Chester MSS. in Coll. Arms, (Devon.) i. 53.
LLANTRITHYD. The Registers of Llantrithyd, Glamorganshire, 1571-1810. Edited by H. S. Hughes. London, 1888, 8vo.
LONG BREDY. Chester MSS. in Coll. Arms, (Dorset,) 211.
LONG BURTON. Chester MSS. in Coll. Arms, (Dorset,) 31-40.
LONG DITTON. Chester MSS. in Coll. Arms, (Surrey,) iv. 233.
LONG MELFORD. Parker's History of Long Melford, 359. Chester MSS. in Coll. Arms, (Suffolk,) 215.
LONG NEWTON. Chronicon Mirabile, or Extracts from Parish Registers, 152.
LONG SUTTON, or SUTTON ST. MARY. Chester MSS. in Coll. Arms, (Lincolnshire,) ii. 269 ; v. 335.
LOUGHBOROUGH. The Rectors of Loughborough, by W. G. D. Fletcher, 47. The Reliquary, xiii. 191.

LOUGHTON (Essex). MS. in Coll. Arms, J. P. cxciii. 159.

LOUTH. Chester MSS. in Coll. Arms, (Lincolnshire,) i. 179-196; ii. 376.

LOWICK (co. Northampton). MS. in Coll. Arms, R. B. G. xxiii., 126.

LUCCOMBE. Chester MSS. in Coll. Arms, (Somerset,) ii. 7.

LUDBOROUGH. Chester MSS. in Coll. Arms, (Lincolnshire,) i. 177.

LUTON. Blades' Genealogia Bedfordiensis, 181-190. Chester MSS. in Coll. Arms, (Bedfordshire,) 313.

LYME REGIS. Chester MSS. in Coll. Arms, (Dorset,) 261.

LYMINGTON. MS. in Coll. Arms, J. P. cxciii. 423.

LYMM. Chester MSS. in Coll. Arms, (Cheshire,) 75-88.

LYNTON. Chester MSS. in Coll. Arms, (Devon,) i. 41.

LONDON AND MIDDLESEX:

ACTON. Chester MSS. in Coll. Arms, (Middlesex,) i. 303-352.

ALL HALLOWS BARKING. Notes and Queries, 3 S. ii. 423, 441; iii. 61, 162, 323. Chester MSS. in Coll. Arms, (London,) viii. 1-189.

ALL HALLOWS BREAD STREET. Malcolm's Londinum Redivivum, ii. 12.

ALL HALLOWS THE GREAT. Chester MSS. in Coll. Arms, (London,) xii. 156-178.

ALL HALLOWS HONEY LANE. Malcolm's Londinum Redivivum, ii. 163.

ALL HALLOWS THE LESS. Chester MSS. in Coll. Arms, (London,) xii. 117-155.

ALL HALLOWS LOMBARD STREET. Complete copy, 1550-1867. Chester MSS. in Coll. Arms, (London,) vii. Malcolm's Londinum Redivivum, i. 55.

ALL HALLOWS LONDON WALL. Edited by E. B. Jupp and Robert Hovenden, 1559-1675. London, 1878, 4to. MS. in Coll. Arms, J. P. clxxxviii. 75.

ALL HALLOWS STAINING. Malcolm's Londinum Redivivum, ii. 27. Chester MSS. in Coll. Arms, (London,) x. 283-372.

ALL HALLOWS THAMES STREET. Malcolm's Londinum Redivivum, i. 44.

BERMONDSEY, ST. MARY MAGDALEN. Commencing in 1548. In course of publication in the Genealogist, New Series.

BOW. Hare's Miscell. Par. Registers, MS. in Coll. Arms, 200.

BRIDEWELL HOSPITAL CHAPEL. Chester MSS. in Coll. Arms, (Private Chapels,) 263.

BUNHILL FIELDS. Register of Burials, 1713-1826. MSS. in Coll. Arms, 6 vols.

CHAPEL ROYAL, WHITEHALL. Complete transcript, 1704-1867. Chester MSS. in Coll. Arms, (Private Chapels).

CHAPELS ROYAL. Chester MSS. in Coll. Arms, (Private Chapels).

CHELSEA. Faulkner's Description of Chelsea, 108-123. All the Marriages, 1559-1754; extracts after, and of Births and Deaths. Chester MSS. in Coll. Arms, (Middlesex,) i 19-302.

CHELSEA HOSPITAL. Chester MSS. in Coll. Arms, (Private Chapels,) 325-356.

LONDON AND MIDDLESEX—*continued :*

CHISWICK. Chester MSS. in Coll. Arms, (Middlesex,) ii. 99-177.

CHRIST CHURCH FARRINGDON WITHIN. Malcolm's Londinum Redivivum, iii. 337.

CHRIST CHURCH NEWGATE. Chester MSS. in Coll. Arms, (London,) iii. 221-254.

CLERKENWELL. *See* ST. JAMES.

DUKE STREET CHAPEL, WESTMINSTER. Collectanea Topographica et Genealogica, iii. 382.

DUTCH CHURCH, AUSTIN FRIARS. 1571-1874. Edited by W. J. C. Moens. Lymington, 1884, 8vo.

EALING. Ealing St. Mary's Monthly Church Paper, Nos. 1-12, 1884, 8vo. MS. in Coll. Arms, J. P. cxcv. 89.

FLEET REGISTERS. Burn's History of Fleet Marriages, 2nd edition, 71-126. Chester MSS. in Coll. Arms, (Private Chapels,) 283-324.

GRAY'S INN CHAPEL. Register of Marriages, printed in Joseph Foster's 'Collectanea Genealogica.' Chester MSS. in Coll. Arms, (Private Chapels,) 39.

HACKNEY. Chester MSS. in Coll. Arms, (Middlesex,) iii. 1-225.

HAMMERSMITH. Collectanea Topographica et Genealogica, iii. 316.

HAMPSTEAD. Chester MSS. in Coll. Arms, (Middlesex,) i. 24.

KENSINGTON, ST. MARY ABBOTS. Extracts in the St. Mary Abbots' Parish Magazine. (In progress.)

HIGHGATE. Chester MSS. in Coll. Arms, (Middlesex,) i. 4.

ISLINGTON, ST. MARY. MS. in Coll. Arms, J. P. cxcv. 109.

LAMBETH. Hare's Miscell. Par. Registers, MS. in Coll. Arms, 183.

LAMBS' CHAPEL, or ST. JAMES-ON-THE-WALL. Chester MSS. in Coll. Arms. (Private Chapels,) 237.

LINCOLN'S INN CHAPEL. Chester MSS. in Coll. Arms, (Private Chapels,) 377-392.

MAY FAIR. Burn's History of Fleet Marriages, 2nd edition, 148.

MERCER'S CHAPEL. Complete transcript, 1641-1833. Chester MSS. in Coll. Arms, (Private Chapels).

OXFORD CHAPEL. Chester MSS. in Coll. Arms, (Private Chapels,) 233.

ROLLS CHAPEL. Collectanea Topographica et Genealogica, iii. 384. Complete transcript, 1736-1826. Chester MSS. in Coll. Arms, (Private Chapels,) 231.

ST. ALBAN, WOOD STREET. Malcolm's Londinum Redivivum, ii. 310. Chester MSS. in Coll. Arms, (London,) ii. 219-244.

ST. ALPHAGE. Malcolm's Londinum Redivivum, i. 23.

ST. ALPHAGE, LONDON WALL. Hare's Miscell. Par. Registers, MS. in Coll. Arms, 223. Chester MSS. in Coll. Arms, (London,) v. 135-192.

ST. ANDREW BAYNARD CASTLE. Malcolm's Londinum Redivivum, ii. 365.

ST. ANDREW HOLBORN. Notes and Queries, 2 S. xii. 227, 430. Malcolm's Londinum Redivivum, ii. 202. A MS. containing very extensive extracts is in Coll. Arms, made by G. E. Cokayne, Esq., Norroy. 2 vols. 4to.

LONDON AND MIDDLESEX—*continued :*

ST. ANDREW WARDROBE. Hare's Miscell. Par. Registers, MS. in Coll. Arms, 153. Chester MSS. in Coll. Arms, (London,) iv. 295-333. MS. in Coll. Arms, J. P. cxcv. 91, 105.

ST. ANDREW UNDERSHAFT. Malcolm's Londinum Redivivum, i. 70. MS. in Coll. Arms, J. P. cxcv. 107.

ST. ANNE BLACKFRIARS. Malcolm's Londinum Redivivum, ii. 366. Hare's Miscell. Par. Registers, MS. in Coll. Arms, 150. Chester MSS. in Coll. Arms, (London,) iv. 235-293.

ST. ANNE SOHO. Chester MSS. in Coll. Arms, (Westminster,) viii.

ST. ANTHOLIN, AND ST JOHN BAPTIST-ON-WALLBROOK. Vol. viii. of Publications of the Harleian Society. Register Section. Partly edited by Joseph Lemuel Chester, and completed by Geo. J. Armytage. St. Antholin, Baptisms, Marriages, and Burials, 1538-1754 ; St. John Baptist, Baptisms, 1682-1754, Burials, 1686-1754.

ST. AUGUSTINE. Malcolm's Londinum Redivivum, ii. 93. Chester MSS. in Coll. Arms, (London,) v. 251-324.

ST. BARTHOLEMEW EXCHANGE. Chester MSS. in Coll. Arms, (London,) vi. 193-288.

ST. BARTHOLEMEW THE GREAT. Malcolm's Londinum Redivivum, ii. 428. Chester MSS. in Coll. Arms, (London,) vi. 289-358.

ST. BARTHOLOMEW THE LESS. Malcolm's Londinum Redivivum, i. 305. Chester MSS. in Coll. Arms, (London,) viii. 237-307.

ST. BENET FINK. Malcolm's Londinum Redivivum, ii. 463. Chester MSS. in Coll. Arms, (London,) iv. 365-386 ; xii. 1-31. MS. in Coll. Arms, J. P. clxxxviii. 119.

ST. BENET GRACECHURCH. Complete transcript, 1558 - 1866. Chester MSS. in Coll. Arms, (London,) ix.

ST. BENNET PAUL'S WHARF. Hare's Miscell. Par. Registers, MS. in Coll. Arms, 217. Chester MSS. in Coll. Arms, (London,) iii. 1-83. MS. in Coll. Arms, R. B. G. xxiii. 79, 154 ; xxxix. 6. MS. in Coll. Arms, J. P. clxxxviii. 30, 84.

ST. BOTOLPH ALDGATE. MSS. in Coll. Arms, J. P. clxxxviii. 27, 60 ; J. P. cxcv. 87.

ST. BOTOLPH BISHOPSGATE. The Registers of St. Botolph, Bishopsgate, 1558-1753. Transcribed by A. W. C. Hallen. London, 1886. 2 vols., 8vo.

ST. BRIDE'S. Malcolm's Londinum Redivivum, i. 364. Chester MSS. in Coll. Arms, (London,) iv. 1-232.

ST. CATHARINE CREE CHURCH. Malcolm's Londinum Redivivum, iii. 319.

ST. CHRISTOPHER-LE-STOCKS. The Register Book of the Parish of St. Christopher-le Stocks. Edited by Edwin Freshfield. 1558-1781. London, 1882, 4to. Three vols.

ST. CLEMENT DANES. MS. in Coll. Arms, Registers J. W. 89-108. MS. in Coll. Arms, J. P. clxxxviii. 158.

LONDON AND MIDDLESEX—*continued* :

ST. DIONIS BACKCHURCH. 1538-1754. Vol. iii. of Publications of the Harleian Society, Register Section. Edited by Joseph Lemuel Chester. Hare's Miscell. Par. Registers, MS. in Coll. Arms, 213.

ST. DUNSTAN-IN-THE EAST. Chester MSS. in Coll. Arms, (London,) xii. 33-116. MS. in Coll. Arms, J. P. cxcv. 66.

ST. DUNSTAN-IN-THE-WEST. Collectanea Topographica et Genealogica, iv. 116 ; v. 202, 365. Malcolm's Londinum Redivivum, iii. 459. MS. in Coll. Arms, J. P. clxxxviii. 268.

ST. FAITH. Malcolm's Londinum Redivivum, ii. 110. Chester MSS. in Coll. Arms, (London,) v. 327-389.

ST. GEORGE BLOOMSBURY. Chester MSS. in Coll. Arms, (Middlesex,) iv. 221-32-.

ST. GEORGE HANOVER SQUARE. Vols. xi. and xiv. of Publications of the Harleian Society, Register Section. Marriages, 1725-1809. Edited by J. H. Chapman.

ST. GEORGE THE MARTYR, QUEEN'S SQUARE. Printed in the St. George's Parish Magazine, beginning in the No. for March, 1888, 4to. (In progress.)

ST. GILES CRIPPLEGATE. Chester MSS. in Coll. Arms, (London,) i. ii. Hare's Miscell. Par. Registers, MS. in Coll. Arms, 211. MS. in Coll. Arms, Registers, J. W. 121-192. Malcolm's Londinum Redivivum, iii. 285-301.

ST. GILES-IN-THE-FIELDS. The Genealogist, ii. 383. Chester MSS. in Coll. Arms, (Middlesex,) iv. 1-206.

ST. GREGORY-BY-ST. PAUL'S. Chester MSS. in Coll. Arms, (London,) iii. 309-338. MS. in Coll. Arms, J. P. cxcvi. 1.

ST. HELEN BISHOPSGATE. Annals of St. Helen's, Bishopsgate, by J. E. Cox, 91-99. Malcolm's Londinum Redivivum, iii. 558. Chester MSS. in Coll. Arms, (London,) xi. 1-177.

ST. JAMES CLERKENWELL. Vols. ix. x. and xiii. of Publications of the Harleian Society, Register Section. Edited by Robert Hovenden. Baptisms and Marriages, 1551-1754. Malcolm's Londinum Redivivum, iii. 215. Hare's Miscell. Par. Registers, MS. in Coll. Arms, 189.

ST. JAMES ON-THE-WALL. See LAMBS' CHAPEL.

ST. JAMES, WESTMINSTER. Nichols' Topographer, iii. 491. Chester MSS. in Coll. Arms, (Westminster,) viii. ix.

ST. JOHN BAPTIST-ON-WALLBROOK. See ST. ANTHOLIN.

ST. JOHN'S CHAPEL, BEDFORD Row. Collectanea Topographica et Genealogica, iii. 386.

ST. JOHN EVANGELIST, WATLING STREET. Hare's Miscell. Par. Registers, MS. in Coll. Arms, 227.

ST. JOHN EVANGELIST, WESTMINSTER. Chester MSS. in Coll. Arms, (Westminster,) x.

ST. LAURENCE POUNTNEY. Wilson's History of St. Laurence Pountney, 129. Chester MSS. in Coll. Arms, (London,) v. 195-249.

ST. LAWRENCE JEWRY. Chester MSS. in Coll. Arms, (London,) iii. 257-291.

LONDON AND MIDDLESEX—*continued*:

St. Leonard East Cheap. Complete transcript, 1538 - 1812.
Malcolm's Londinum Redivivum, i. 324. Chester MSS. in Coll.
Arms, (London,) ix.

St. Leonard Foster Lane. Chester MSS. in Coll. Arms,
(London,) iii. 221-254.

St. Margaret Lothbury. Chester MSS. in Coll. Arms, (London,)
vi. 1-87.

St. Martin-in-the-Fields. Chester MSS. in Coll. Arms, (Westminster,) vi. vii.

St. Martin Ironmonger Lane. Chester MSS. in Coll. Arms,
(London,) vii. 381.

St. Martin Ludgate. Malcolm's Londinum Redivivum, iv. 357.

St. Martin Outwich. Chester MSS. in Coll. Arms, (London,)
ii. 363-374 ; xi. 375-401.

St. Mary Abchurch. Chester MSS. in Coll. Arms, (London.) ii.
333-362.

St. Mary Aldermanbury. Malcolm's Londinum Redivivum,
ii. 128. Chester MSS. in Coll. Arms, (London,) v. 1-132.

St. Mary Aldermary. 1558-1754. Vol. v. of Publications of
the Harleian Society, Register Section. Edited by Joseph
Lemuel Chester. Chester MSS. in Coll. Arms, (London,)
iii. 109-147.

St. Mary le Bone. Chester MSS. in Coll. Arms, (Middlesex,) ii.
65-97.

St. Mary le Bow. Malcolm's Londinum Redivivum, ii. 156.
Hare's Miscell. Par. Registers, MS. in Coll. Arms, 212

St. Mary Cole Abbey. Hare's Miscell. Par. Registers, MS. in
Coll. Arms. 128.

St. Mary Colechurch. History of the Church of St. Mildred
the Virgin, Poultry, by Thomas Milbourn, 61-65, 77.

St. Mary Magdalen, Milk Street. Chester MSS. in Coll. Arms,
(London,) iii. 293-307.

,,   ,,   Old Fish Street. Chester MSS. in Coll.
Arms, (London,) iii. 341.

St. Mary le Strand. The Genealogist, New Series, iv. 34. 108 ;
v. 108. (Weddings only, 1605-1625).

St. Mary Whitechapel. Malcolm's Londinum Redivivum, iv.
457. New York Record, xix. 103, etc., Weddings, 1606-1625.

St. Mary Woolchurch Haw. See St. Mary Woolnoth.

St. Mary Woolnoth. The Registers of St. Mary Woolnoth and
St. Mary Woolchurch Haw, 1538-1760. By J. M. S. Brooke and
A. W. C. Hallen. London, 1886, 8vo.

St. Matthew, Friday Street. Malcolm's Londinum Redivivum,
iv. 439. History of St. Matthew Friday Street, and St. Peter
Cheap, by W. S. Simpson, 33. Chester MSS. in Coll. Arms,
(London,) 169-186.

St. Michael Cornhill. 1546-1754. Vol. vii. of Publications of
the Harleian Society, Register Section. Partly edited by Joseph
Lemuel Chester.

LONDON AND MIDDLESEX—*continued*:

ST. MICHAEL ROYAL. Hare's Miscell. Par. Registers, MS. in Coll. Arms, 155a. Chester MSS. in Coll. Arms, (London,) xii. 179-215.

ST. MILDRED POULTRY. History of the Church of St. Mildred the Virgin, Poultry, by Thomas Milbourn, 27-37, 82.

ST. NICHOLAS ACON. The Register Book of St. Nicholas Acons, London, 1539-1812. Transcribed by William Brigg. Leeds, 1890, fol.

ST. NICHOLAS COLE ABBEY. Hare's Miscell. Par. Registers, MS. in Coll. Arms, 131.

ST. OLAVE HART STREET. Collectanea Topographica et Genealogica, ii. 311. Chester MSS. in Coll. Arms, (London,) xi. 179-374.

ST. OLAVE JEWRY. Chester MSS. in Coll. Arms, (London,) vii. 351-373.

ST. OLAVE SILVER STREET. Chester MSS. in Coll. Arms, (London,) ii. 245-264.

ST. PANCRAS SOPER LANE. Malcolm's Londinum Redivivum, ii. 171.

ST. PAUL'S CATHEDRAL. Chester MSS. in Coll. Arms, (London,) iii. 349.

ST. PAUL COVENT GARDEN. Chronicon Mirabile, or Extracts from Parish Registers, 146. Chester MSS. in Coll. Arms, (Westminster,) x.

ST. PETER CHEAP. Chester MSS. in Coll. Arms, (London,) iii. 189-219.

ST. PETER CORNHILL. Vols. i. and iv. of Publications of the Harleian Society. Register Section. Edited by Granville W. G. Leveson Gower. Baptisms and Burials, 1538-1774 ; Marriages, 1538-1754.

ST. PETER PAUL'S WHARF. Hare's Miscell. Par. Registers, MS. in Coll. Arms, 209. Chester MSS. in Coll. Arms, (London,) iii. 85-108. MS. in Coll. Arms, J. P. clxxxviii. 126, 141.

ST. PETER-LE-POOR. Chester MSS. in Coll. Arms, (London,) iv. 335-362 ; viii. 309-389. MS. in Coll. Arms. J. P. clxxxviii. 23.

ST. PETER AD VINCULA. Notices of the Historic Persons buried in the Chapel of St. Peter ad Vincula in the Tower of London, by D. C. Bell, 42-49. Chester MSS. in Coll. Arms, (London,) viii. 191-235.

ST. SEPULCHRE. Chester MSS. in Coll. Arms, (London,) ii. 265-332.

ST. STEPHEN COLEMAN STREET. MS. in Coll. Arms, J. P. clxxxviii. 76 ; J. P. excv. 64.

ST. STEPHEN WALBROOK. Hare's Miscell. Par. Registers, MS. in Coll. Arms, 203. MS. in Coll. Arms, J. P. excv. 78.

ST. SWITHIN LONDON STONE. Hare's Miscell. Par. Registers, MS. in Coll. Arms, 205.

ST. THOMAS THE APOSTLE. Vol. vi. of Publications of the Harleian Society. Register Section. Edited by Joseph Lemuel Chester. Baptisms and Burials, 1558-1754 ; Marriages, 1558-1672.

3

LONDON AND MIDDLESEX—*continued* :

SAVOY CHAPEL. Chester MSS. in Coll. Arms, (Private Chapels,) 27.

SHOREDITCH. Chester MSS. in Coll. Arms, (Middlesex,) i. 45-128.

SOMERSET HOUSE. Marriages, Baptisms, and Burials, which have been solemnized in the Private Chapel of Somerset House, Strand, in the county of Middlesex. Extending from 1714-1776. London, printed for James Coleman, 1862, 8vo. This was previously privately printed by Sir Thomas Phillipps, in 1831, 8vo.

SPITALFIELDS. *See* WHEELER CHAPEL.

STAINES. The Parish Registers of Staines, co. Middlesex, 1644-1694. Privately printed for F. A. Crisp, 1887, fol. Original Register of Baptisms and Burials, 1653-1691 ; Marriages, 1653-1660, in British Museum, Egerton MS. 2004.

STOKE NEWINGTON. Chester MSS. in Coll. Arms, (Middlesex,) ii. 1-63.

TEMPLE CHURCH. Complete transcript. Chester MSS. in Coll. Arms, (Private Chapels,) 57.

TWICKENHAM. Memorials of Twickenham. by R. S. Cobbett, 47-82. Chester MSS. in Coll. Arms, (Middlesex,) ii. 179-217. Chronicon Mirabile, or Extracts from Parish Registers, 138.

WESTMINSTER ABBEY. 1606-1875. Vol. x. of Publications of the Harleian Society. Edited by Joseph Lemuel Chester.

„ ST. MARGARET. Complete transcript. Chester MSS. in Coll. Arms, (Westminster,) ii. iii. iv. v. History of the Parish Church of St. Margaret, by M. E. C. Walcott, 35-47.

WESTMINSTER. *See* DUKE STREET CHAPEL, ST. JAMES.

WHEELER CHAPEL, SPITALFIELDS. Collectanea Topographica et Genealogica, iii. 388.

MABLETHORPE. Chester MSS. in Coll. Arms, (Lincolnshire,) i. 170.

MACCLESFIELD. The Registers of Macclesfield, in the Macclesfield Parish Magazine, commencing with the No. for February, 1886, 4to. (In progress.)

MADRON. The First Book of the Parish Registers of Madron. Edited by George Bown Millett. Penzance, 1877, 4to. Baptisms, 1592-1726 ; Marriages, 1577-1678 ; Burials, 1577-1681.

MAIDSTONE. The Registers of All Saints, Maidstone, from the year 1542. Edited by J. Cave-Browne. London, 1890, 8vo. (In progress.) Chester MSS. in Coll. Arms, (Kent,) ii. 133.

MAIDWELL. MS. in Coll. Arms, R. B. G. xxiii. 136.

MAKER. Heraldic Church Notes from Cornwall, by A. J. Jewers, 190-209.

MALMESBURY. Collectanea Topographica et Genealogica, vi. 237. Chester MSS. in Coll. Arms, (Wilts,) 1.

MALTBY-LE-MARSH. Chester MSS. in Coll. Arms, (Lincolnshire,) i. 317.

MANBY. Chester MSS. in Coll. Arms, (Lincolnshire,) iii. 377.

MANSFIELD. British Museum, Add. MSS. 21569, 24591. Chester MSS. in Coll. Arms, (Notts,) ii. 149 274.

MAPERTON. Chester MSS. in Coll. Arms, (Somerset,) i. 269.
MAPLETON. Chester MSS. in Coll. Arms, (Derbyshire,) i. 271.
MARGARET RODING. The Genealogist, New Series, vi. 12.
MARKBY. Chester MSS. in Coll. Arms, (Lincolnshire,) ii. 28.
MARKET CELL (Parish of Caddington, co. Bedford). Church Notes
 and Registers, MS. in Coll. Arms, 26.
MARKET DEEPING. Chester MSS. in Coll. Arms, (Lincolnshire,) i. 7.
MARKET LAVINGTON. Collectanea Topographica et Genealogica, viii.
 201.
MARKET RASEN. Chester MSS. in Coll. Arms, (Lincolnshire,) v. 49.
MARLBOROUGH, ST. MARY. Collectanea Topographica et Genealogica,
 v. 268. Chester MSS. in Coll. Arms, (Wilts,) 33.
   " SS. PETER AND PAUL. Collectanea Topographica et
 Genealogica, v. 260. Chester MSS. in Coll. Arms, (Wilts,) 15.
MARSHAM. The Parish Register of Marsham, Norfolk, 1538-1836.
 Edited by A. T. Michell. Norwich, 1889, 8vo.
MARSH BALDON. Chester MSS. in Coll. Arms, (Oxfordshire,) ii.
 289.
MARSH CHAPEL. Chester MSS. in Coll. Arms, (Lincolnshire,) i. 300.
MARSHFIELD. Parish Registers, Glouc., MS. in Coll. Arms, R. B. G.
 xxii. fol. 162.
MARSTON-MONTGOMERY. The Reliquary, vii. 140.
MARSTON-MORTEYNE. Blades' Genealogia Bedfordiensis, 191.
MARSWORTH. Church Notes and Registers, MS. in Coll. Arms, 8.
MARTOCK. Chester MSS. in Coll. Arms, (Somerset,) i. 265.
MARTON. Chester MSS. in Coll. Arms, (Lincolnshire,) i. 220.
MASSINGHAM. Hare's Miscell. Par. Registers, MS. in Coll. Arms,
 173.
MATSON. MS. in Coll. Arms, R. B. G. xxxviii. 10.
MAULDEN. Blades' Genealogia Bedfordiensis, 194.
MEDMENHAM. Chester MSS. in Coll. Arms, (Bucks,) 63.
MELBOURNE. Chester MSS. in Coll. Arms, (Derbyshire,) i. 23.
MELBURY OSMOND. Chester MSS. in Coll. Arms, (Dorset,) 63.
MELBURY SAMPFORD. Chester MSS. in Coll. Arms, (Dorset,) 61.
MELCHBOURNE. Blades' Genealogia Bedfordiensis, 199.
MELLS. Chester MSS. in Coll. Arms, (Somerset,) iii. 45.
MEPPERSALL. Blades' Genealogia Bedfordiensis, 201.
MEREWORTH. Chronicon Mirabile, or Extracts from Parish Registers,
 134.
MERRINGTON. Chronicon Mirabile, or Extracts from Parish Registers,
 20.
MERSTHAM. Chester MSS. in Coll. Arms, (Surrey,) ii. 339.
MERTON. Chester MSS. in Coll. Arms, (Surrey,) iii. 199.
MERTON. Chester MSS. in Coll. Arms, (Oxfordshire,) iii. 109, 279.
MESSING. Chester MSS. in Coll. Arms, (Essex,) i. 13.
MESSINGHAM. Chester MSS. in Coll. Arms, (Lincolnshire,) i. 241.
MICKLETON. Mickleton Register of Marriages, 1594-1736. Privately
 printed by Sir Thos. Phillpps, N.D. pp. 4, 8vo. Chester MSS. in
 Coll. Arms, (Gloucestershire,) 11, 161-171. MS. in Coll. Arms,
 R. B. G. xxxviii. 20.

MIDDLE CLAYDON. Chester MSS. in Coll. Arms, (Bucks,) 69.

MIDDLE RASEN. Chester MSS. in Coll. Arms, (Lincolnshire,) iv. 143.

MIDDLETON. Lanc. and Cheshire Antiquarian Notes, i. 141.

   ,,   ST. GEORGE. Chronicon Mirabile, or Extracts from Parish Registers, 87.

   ,,   STONEY. Chester MSS. in Coll. Arms, (Oxfordshire,) i. 383.

MILDENHALL. Collectanea Topographica et Genealogica, v. 350.

MILLBROOKE. Blades' Genealogia Bedfordiensis, 203.

MILTON BRYAN. Blades' Genealogia Bedfordiensis, 205.

MILTON ERNEST. A complete transcript of vol. i. of the Register, 1538-1678. Chester MSS. in Coll. Arms, (Bedfordshire,) 37-92. Blades' Genealogia Bedfordiensis, 208.

MILTON LISLEBON. Nichols' Topographer, iii. 347.

MINEHEAD. Chester MSS. in Coll. Arms, (Somerset,) ii. 135.

MINETY. MS. in Coll. Arms, R. B. G. xxxviii. 31.

MINTERNE MAGNA. Chester MSS. in Coll. Arms, (Dorset,) 161-172.

MINTING. Chester MSS. in Coll. Arms, (Lincolnshire,) ii. 142.

MITCHAM. Complete transcript 1563-1678, and extracts after. Chester MSS. in Coll. Arms, (Surrey,) iii. 1-157, 203-306. The Reliquary, xviii. 1, 136 ; xix. 17, 231 ; xx. 44.

MITCHELL DEAN. MS. in Coll. Arms, R. B. G. xxxviii. 23.

MOLLINGTON. Chester MSS. in Coll. Arms, (Oxfordshire,) ii. 129.

MONKLEIGH. Chester MSS. in Coll. Arms, (Devon,) iv. 157-186.

MONKTON (co. Somerset). MS. in Coll. Arms, J. P. cxcii. 322.

MONYASH. The Reliquary, v. 85.

MORDEN. The Genealogist, vii. 33. Chester MSS. in Coll. Arms, (Surrey,) ii. 309-338. MS. in Coll. Arms, J. P. cxciii. 261.

MORLEY. See TOPCLIFFE.

MORTON-NEAR-BOURN. Chester MSS. in Coll. Arms, (Lincolnshire,) ii. 117.

MOTTRAM. Chester MSS. in Coll. Arms, (Cheshire,) 147-160.

MOULTON. Chester MSS. in Coll. Arms, (Lincolnshire,) ii. 44 ; v. 307.

MUCH WENLOCK. Extracts from the Registers of Sir Thomas Butler, Vicar of Much Wenlock, 1539-1560. Edited by Rev. C. H. Hartshorne. Tenby, 1861, 8vo. This register was burnt.

MUMBY. Chester MSS. in Coll. Arms, (Lincolnshire,) iii. 391 ; iv. 369.

MUTHILL. The Register of Baptisms, Muthill, Perthshire, from 1697-1847. Edited by A. W. C. Hallen. Edinburgh, 1887, 8vo.

NAILSEA. Chester MSS. in Coll. Arms, (Somerset,) i. 41.

NANTWICH. James Hall's History of Nantwich, 336-353. Chester MSS. in Coll. Arms, (Cheshire,) 137.

NARBOROUGH (co. Northampton). MS. in Coll. Arms, R. B. G. xxiii. 117.

NAVESTOCK. Chester MSS. in Coll. Arms, (Essex,) iii. 125-148.

NAZING. Chester MSS. in Coll. Arms, (Essex,) iii. 361.

NETHER WORTON. Chester MSS. in Coll. Arms, (Oxfordshire,) i. 201.

NETTLEDEN. Church Notes and Registers, MS. in Coll. Arms, 27.

NETTLEHAM. Chester MSS. in Coll. Arms, (Lincolnshire,) v. 331.

NEWARK-ON-TRENT. Chester MSS. in Coll. Arms, (Notts,) i. 185-274.

NEWBURY. Chester MSS. in Coll. Arms (Berkshire,) 173-189.

NEWCASTLE-ON-TYNE, ALL SAINTS. Chronicon Mirabile, or Extracts from Parish Registers, 104. Chester MSS. in Coll. Arms, (Northumberland,) 365.

    ,, ST. ANDREW. Chronicon Mirabile, or Extracts from Parish Registers, 91.

    ,, ST. JOHN. Chronicon Mirabile, or Extracts from Parish Registers, 89. Chester MSS. in Coll. Arms, (Northumberland,) 387.

    ,, ST. NICHOLAS. Chronicon Mirabile, or Extracts from Parish Registers, 94. Chester MSS. in Coll. Arms, (Northumberland.) 1-335.

NEWCHURCH. Chester MSS. in Coll. Arms, (Lancashire,) 185.

NEWDEGATE. Chester MSS. in Coll. Arms, (Surrey,) iv. 249. MS. in Coll. Arms, J. P. cxciii. 293.

NEWENT. MS. in Coll. Arms, R. B, G. xxii. 148 ; xxxviii. 8.

NEWINGTON. Chester MSS. in Coll. Arms, (Oxfordshire,) ii. 145.

NEWINTON, ST. MARY. Chester MSS. in Coll. Arms, (Surrey,) ii. 239-284.

NEWPORT. Chester MSS. in Coll. Arms, (Essex,) iii. 193.

NEWPORT PAGNELL. Chester MSS. in Coll. Arms, (Bucks,) 153.

NEW SLEAFORD. Chester MSS. in Coll. Arms, (Lincolnshire,) ii. 191-200.

NEWTON-NEAR-FALKINGHAM. Chester MSS. in Coll. Arms, (Lincolnshire,) i. 267.

NEWTON LINFORD. The Parish Registers of Newton Linford, 1677-1679. Privately printed for F. A. Crisp, 1884, fol.

NEWTON ST. PETROCK. A complete transcript, 1578-1812. Chester MSS. in Coll. Arms, (Devon,) ii. 61-108.

NEWTON-BY-TOFT. Chester MSS. in Coll. Arms, (Lincolnshire,) v. 195.

NEWTON-ON-TRENT. Chester MSS. in Coll. Arms, (Lincolnshire,) ii. 190.

NEYLAND. Chester MSS. in Coll. Arms, (Suffolk,) 303.

NOKE. Chester MSS. in Coll. Arms, (Oxfordshire,) ii. 151 ; iii. 291.

NONINGTON. Chester MSS. in Coll. Arms, (Kent,) ii. 83.

NORBURY. Chester MSS. in Coll. Arms, (Staffordshire,) 13.

NORMANBY-BY-CLAXBY. Chester MSS. in Coll. Arms, (Lincolnshire,) v. 35.

NORMANTON. The Reliquary, ii. 7. British Museum, Add. MS. 24600.

NORRIS. Registers of the Rev. Thomas. The Genealogist, i. 171.

NORTHAMPTON, ST. SEPULCHRE. Chester MSS. in Coll. Arms, (Northampton,) i. 333. MS. in Coll. Arms, R. B. G. xxiii. 133.

    ,, ALL SAINTS. MS. in Coll. Arms, R. B. G. xxiii. 134.

    ,, ST. GILES. MS. in Coll. Arms, R. B. G. xxiii. 134.

NORTH ASTON. Chester MSS. in Coll. Arms, (Oxfordshire,) ii. 271.

NORTHAW. Extracts from the Registers, 4to. page, signed J. E. Cussans, and dated February 28, 1881. The originals were burnt, as well as the church, in February, 1881.

NORTH CADBURY. Chester MSS. in Coll. Arms, (Somerset,) i. 287.

NORTH CHERITON. Chester MSS. in Coll. Arms, (Somerset,) ii. 25.

NORTH COCKERINGTON. Chester MSS. in Coll. Arms, (Lincolnshire,) i. 120.

NORTH COVE. East Anglian, ii. 317.

NORTH CREAKE. Chester MSS. in Coll. Arms, (Norfolk,) i. 1-67.

NORTH ELMHAM. The Ancient Register of North Elmham, 1536-1631. By A. G. Legge, vicar. Norwich, 1888, 8vo.

NORTHENDEN. Chester MSS. in Coll. Arms, (Cheshire.) 171-190.

NORTHILL. Blades' Genealogia Bedfordiensis, 212. Chester MSS. in Coll. Arms, (Bedfordshire,) 17.

NORTHIAM. Chronicon Mirabile, or Extracts from Parish Registers, 154.

NORTH LEIGH. Chester MSS. in Coll. Arms, (Oxfordshire,) ii. 119.

NORTH MOOR. Chester MSS. in Coll. Arms, (Oxfordshire,) ii. 157.

NORTH OCKENDON. Chester MSS. in Coll. Arms, (Essex,) iii. 149-175.

NORTHORPE. Chester MSS. in Coll. Arms, (Lincolnshire,) i. 281.

NORTHOWRAM or COLEY. The Nonconformist Register of Baptisms, Marriages, and Deaths, Compiled by the Revs. Oliver Heywood and T. Dickenson, 1644-1702, 1702-1752, generally known as the Northowram or Coley Register. Edited by J. Horsfall Turner. Brighouse, 1881, 8vo. Heywood's Register is called 'A Register for Coley Chappell,' pp. 17-108. Dickenson's Register, pp. 164-338.

NORTH SOMERCOTES. Chester MSS. in Coll. Arms, (Lincolnshire,) iii. 379.

NORTH THORESBY. Chester MSS. in Coll. Arms, (Lincolnshire,) i. 116; iv. 93.

NORTH WILLINGHAM. Chester MSS. in Coll. Arms, (Lincolnshire,) iv. 129.

NORTH WINFIELD. The Reliquary, xiii. 35, 108.

NORTH WITHAM. Chester MSS. in Coll. Arms, (Lincolnshire,) ii. 108.

NORTH WOOTTON. The Parish Register of North Wootton, Dorset, from the year 1539 to the year 1786. Privately printed by Charles Herbert Mayo. No place or date.

NORTON. Chester MSS. in Coll. Arms, (Derbyshire,) i. 43, 101.

　,, (Durham). Chronicon Mirabile, or Extracts from Parish Registers, 62.

NORWICH. Registers of Walloon Church at Norwich, 1595-1611. Publications of the Huguenot Society, Vol. i., Part ii. Lymington, 1888, 4to.

　,, CATHEDRAL. Chester MSS. in Coll. Arms, (Norfolk,) ii. 149-161.

　,, ST. ANDREW. Chester MSS. in Coll. Arms, (Norfolk,) i. 183.

　,, ST. CLEMENT. The East Anglian, ii. 307.

NORWICH, ST. JOHN MADDERMARKET. The East Anglian, i. 402.
,, ST. MICHAEL-AT-THORNE. The East Anglian, ii. 306.
NOTTINGHAM, ST. MARY. Chester MSS. in Coll. Arms, (Notts,) i. 1-95.
,, ST. PETER. Chester MSS. in Coll. Arms, (Notts,) i. 97-
159.
,, ST. NICHOLAS. Chester MSS. in Coll. Arms, (Notts,)
i. 161-183.
NOWTON. Chester MSS. in Coll. Arms, (Suffolk,) 369.
NUNNEY. Chester MSS. in Coll. Arms, (Somerset,) i. 129 ; ii. 43.
NUTHURST. Baptisms and Burials, 1636. British Museum, Ayscough
MS., 1677. Chester MSS. in Coll. Arms, (Sussex,) i. 103-127.

OAKLEY. Blades' Genealogia Bedfordiensis, 217.
ODCOMBE. Chester MSS. in Coll. Arms, (Somerset,) i. 207-230.
ODDINGTON. Chester MSS. in Coll. Arms, (Oxfordshire,) iii. 295.
ODELL. Blades' Genealogia Bedfordiensis, 220. Harvey's Hundred
of Willey, 372.
ODIHAM. Chester MSS. in Coll. Arms, (Hants,) 159.
OFFENHAM. Chester MSS in Coll. Arms, (Worcestershire,) 109.
OGBOURN ST. ANDREW. Collectanea Topographica et Genealogica,
v. 353.
OLD BASING. Chester MSS. in Coll. Arms, (Hants,) 165.
OLDBURY-ON-SEVERN. Parish Registers, Glouc., MS. in Coll. Arms,
R. B. G. xxii. 138.
OLDHAM. Local Notes and Gleanings. Oldham, 1887, etc., 8vo.,
i. 32 to iii. 64. Complete transcript, 1558-1658. A complete
transcript of the earliest Baptismal Registers, 1558-1611, is in a
MS. in Coll. Arms, fol.
OLD SWINFORD. Chester MSS. in Coll. Arms, (Worcestershire,) 213-
238.
OLVESTON. Chester MSS. in Coll. Arms, (Gloucestershire,) 255.
ONGAR. The Parish Registers of Ongar. 1558-1750. Privately printed
for F. A. Crisp, 1886, fol.
ORMSKIRK. Lancashire and Cheshire Hist. Society, xxvi.
OSBOURNBY. Chester MSS. in Coll. Arms, (Lincolnshire,) i. 264.
OTTON BELCHAMP. Chester MSS. in Coll. Arms, (Essex,) i. 251.
OVER. Notes and Queries, 3 S. iii. 304.
OVER-WORTON. Chester MSS. in Coll. Arms, (Oxfordshire,) i. 205.
OWERSBY. Chester MSS. in Coll. Arms, (Lincolnshire,) v. 41.
OWSTON. Chester MSS. in Coll. Arms, (Lincolnshire,) i. 244.
OXFORD, CHRISTCHURCH. Complete transcript, 1633-1884. Miscel-
lanea Genealogica et Heraldica, 2nd series, i. 143.
,, ALL SAINTS. Complete transcript, 1559-1866. Chester MSS.
in Coll. Arms, (Oxford City,) v.
,, ST. ALDATE. Chester MSS. in Coll. Arms, (Oxford City,)
v. 329-342.
,, ST. EBBES. Chester MSS. in Coll. Arms, (Oxford City,) v.
377.
,, ST. CROSS. Chester MSS. in Coll. Arms, (Oxford City,) v.
361.

OXFORD, ST. GILES. Complete transcript. Chester MSS. in Coll. Arms, (Oxford City,) ii. 181-364.   Marriages, 1599-1754; Baptisms, 1576-1769; Burials, 1605-1768. Extracts after these dates to 1865.

„   ST. JOHN. Chester MSS. in Coll. Arms, (Oxford City,) v. 373.

„   ST. MARTIN. Chester MSS. in Coll. Arms, (Oxford City,) v. 313.

„   ST. MARY MAGDALEN. Chester MSS. in Coll. Arms, (Oxford City,) iv.   Complete transcript, 1600-1726.   Extracts after these dates to 1865, and extracts before 1600 from Rawlinson MSS.

„   „   „   COLLEGE CHAPEL. Chester MSS. in Coll. Arms, (Oxford City,) v. 349.

„   ST. MARY-THE-VIRGIN. Complete transcript, 1599-1866. Chester MSS. in Coll. Arms, (Oxford City,) iii.

„   ST. MICHAEL. Chester MSS. in Coll. Arms, (Oxford City,) v. 289-310.

„   ST. PETER-IN-THE-EAST. Complete transcript, 1559-1866. Chester MSS. in Coll. Arms, (Oxford City.) i. ii.

„   ST. PETER-LE-BAILEY. Chester MSS. in Coll. Arms, (Oxford City,) v. 357.

„   ST. THOMAS. Chester MSS. in Coll. Arms, (Oxford City,) v. 343.

„   WADHAM COLL. CHAPEL. Chester MSS. in Coll. Arms, (Oxford City,) v. 369.

PACKWOOD. Chester MSS. in Coll. Arms, (Warwickshire,) 139.

PADIHAM. The Reliquary, xii. 101.

PAKENHAM. The Parish Registers of Pakenham, Suffolk, 1564-1766. Printed for F. A. Crisp, 1888, fol.

PANNALL. Chester MSS. in Coll. Arms, (Yorkshire,) ii. 181.

PAPWORTH EVERARD (co. Cambridge). Original Register, 1565 1692. British Museum, Add. MS. 31854.

PARKHAM. Complete transcript, 1537-1812. Chester MSS. in Coll. Arms, (Devon,) ii. 109-290.

PASTON. The East Anglian, i. 379.

PAVENHAM. Blades' Genealogia Bedfordiensis, 223.   Harvey's Hundred of Willey, 311.

PEBWORTH. All the Marriages in the Register of Pebworth. co. Gloucester, 1595-1700. Gloucestershire Notes and Queries, Vol. i., pp. 274-279.

PENN. MS. in Coll. Arms, J. P. clxxxvii. 125.

PENWORTHAM. Miscellanea Genealogica et Heraldica, New Series, ii. 205, 221.   Lanc. and Cheshire Antiquarian Notes, ii. 28-33.

PERLETHORPE. The Register of Perlethorpe, 1528-1812.   Edited by George W. Marshall.   Worksop, 1887, fol.

PERTENHALL. Blades' Genealogia Bedfordiensis, 224.

PERTH. Northern Notes and Queries, i. 69, 99, 132, 165; iii. 11, 41, 97; iv. 14.

PETERBOROUGH, CATHEDRAL. Chester MSS. in Coll. Arms, (Northampton,) i. 289.   MS. in Coll. Arms, R. B. G. xxiii. 113.

PETERBOROUGH, ST. JOHN. The old registers of the parish of St. John Baptist, Peterborough, a Lecture, by Rev. W. D. Sweeting. Appendix A. Peterborough, 1881, 8vo. Chester MSS. in Coll. Arms,(Northampton,) i. 323. MS. in Coll. Arms, R. B. G. xxiii. 115.

PETERSHAM. Chester MSS. in Coll. Arms, (Surrey,) iv. 275.

PETROCKSTOWE. Chester MSS. in Coll. Arms, (Devon,) i. 35.

PETWORTH. Chronicon Mirabile, or Extracts from Parish Registers, 148.

PICKENHAM. Hare's Miscell. Par. Registers, MS. in Coll. Arms, 143.

PICKWORTH. Chester MSS. in Coll. Arms, (Lincolnshire,) i. 260.

PILHAM. Chester MSS. in Coll. Arms, (Lincolnshire,) i. 280.

PILTON. Chester MSS. in Coll. Arms, (Northampton,) ii. 117-138.

PINCHBECK. Chester MSS. in Coll. Arms, (Lincolnshire,) i. 134-147.

PIRBRIGHT. MS. in Coll. Arms, J. P. cxciii. 303.

PITCOMBE. Chester MSS. in Coll. Arms, (Somerset,) iii. 143.

PITMINSTER. Chester MSS. in Coll. Arms, (Somerset,) iii. 179.

PITTINGTON. Chronicon Mirabile, or Extracts from Parish Registers, 82.

PLYMOUTH, CHARLES CHURCH. Miscellanea Genealogica et Heraldica, New Series, iv. 167, 175.

PODDINGTON. Blades' Genealogia Bedfordiensis, 226. Harvey's Hundred of Willey, 405.

POOLE. Chester MSS. in Coll. Arms, (Dorset.) 227.

PORLOCK. Chester MSS. in Coll. Arms, (Somerset,) ii. 11.

PORTCHESTER. Chester MSS. in Coll. Arms, (Hants,) 125.

PORTSEA. Chester MSS. in Coll. Arms, (Hants,) 85.

PORTSLADE. Chester MSS. in Coll. Arms, (Sussex,) i. 14, 35, 291.

PORTSMOUTH. Chester MSS. in Coll. Arms, (Hants,) 1-83.

POTTER GROVE. Blades' Genealogia Bedfordiensis, 228.

POTTON. Blades' Genealogia Bedfordiensis, 229.

POUGHILL. Chester MSS. in Coll. Arms, (Cornwall,) 1-30.

PRESHUTE. Collectanea Topographica et Genealogica, v. 346. Chester MSS. in Coll. Arms, (Wilts,) 27.

PRESTBURY. The Register Book of Christenings, Weddings, and Burials, within the Parish of Prestbury, in the County of Chester, 1560-1636. Edited by James Croston, F.S.A. 1881, 8vo. Vol. v. of the publications of the (Lancashire and Cheshire) Record Society.

PRESTON. Chester MSS. in Coll. Arms, (Sussex,) i. 275.

PRESTON-BY-FEVERSHAM. Chester MSS. in Coll. Arms, (Kent,) ii. 147.

PRIORS' DEAN. The Parish Register of Priors' Dean and Colmer to the end of the year 1812. Edited by Thomas Hervey. Colmer, 1886, 4to.

PRITTLEWELL. Chester MSS. in Coll. Arms, (Essex,) iii. 395.

PUCKLECHURCH. Gloucestershire Notes and Queries, iii. 67.

PULLOXHILL. Blades' Genealogia Bedfordiensis, 232.

PURLEIGH. Chester MSS. in Coll. Arms, (Essex,) i. 246.

PUTNEY. Chester MSS. in Coll. Arms, (Surrey,) ii. 1-151.

PUTTENHAM. Chester MSS. in Coll. Arms, (Surrey,) iv. 269.

PUXTON. Chester MSS. in Coll. Arms, (Somerset,) iii. 127.

PYTCHLEY. MS. in Coll. Arms, R. B. G. xxiii. 125.

QUADRING. Chester MSS. in Coll. Arms, (Lincolnshire,) i. 365.
QUATFORD. Original (Bishops') transcripts, 1636-1811. British Museum, Add. MS. 28740.
QUEDGELEY. Chester MSS. in Coll. Arms, (Gloucestershire,) 107-122.
QUINTON. Excerpta ex Registris Parochialibus in Com. Gloucester. Middle Hill, 1854, fol. Chester MSS. in Coll. Arms, (Gloucestershire,) 143.

RADBORNE. MS. in Coll. Arms, J. P. clxxxvii. 175.
RADFORD. The Genealogist, iii. 152.
RAINHAM. Hare's Miscell. Par. Registers, MS. in Coll. Arms, 147. Chester MSS. in Coll. Arms, (Essex,) i. 340.
RAME. Heraldic Church Notes from Cornwall, by A. J. Jewers, 9.
RAMSBURY. Chester MSS. in Coll. Arms, (Wilts,) 107.
RANBY. Chester MSS. in Coll. Arms, (Lincolnshire,) ii. 138.
RAND. Chester MSS. in Coll. Arms, (Lincolnshire,) i. 290.
RAVENSDEN. Blades' Genealogia Bedfordiensis, 234.
RAVENFIELD. British Museum, Add. MS. 24469.
READING, ST. GILES. Chester MSS. in Coll. Arms, (Berkshire,) 337.
      ,, ST. LAWRENCE. Chester MSS. in Coll. Arms, (Berkshire,) 111, 315.
      ,, ST. MARY. Chester MSS. in Coll. Arms, (Berkshire,) 325.
REDENHALL-WITH-HARLESTON. The East Anglian, iv. 150. Chester MSS. in Coll. Arms, (Norfolk,) i. 215.
REDGRAVE. Chester MSS. in Coll. Arms, (Suffolk,) 1-10.
REEPHAM. Chester MSS. in Coll. Arms, (Lincolnshire,) ii. 22.
REIGATE. Chester MSS. in Coll. Arms, (Surrey,) iv. 211.
RENHOLD. Blades' Genealogia Bedfordiensis, 236.
REYMERSTON. Chester MSS. in Coll. Arms, (Norfolk,) i. 375. MS. in Coll. Arms, J. P. cxcvi. 5.
RIBBESFORD. J. R. Burton's History of Bewdley, App. iii.
RIBCHESTER. History of Ribchester, by T. C. Smith and J. Shortt, 189-204.
RIBY. Chester MSS. in Coll. Arms, (Lincolnshire,) iv. 49.
RICHMOND. Chronicon Mirabile, or Extracts from Parish Registers, 122. Chester MSS. in Coll. Arms, (Surrey,) i. 191-297.
RICKMANSWORTH. Chester MSS. in Coll. Arms, (Herts,) ii. 189.
RIDGMONT. Blades' Genealogia Bedfordiensis, 239. Chester MSS. in Coll. Arms, (Bedfordshire,) 1.
RIGSBY. Chester MSS. in Coll. Arms, (Lincolnshire,) iv. 359.
RINGWOLD. Original (Bishops') transcripts, 1636. British Museum, Add. MS. 32344.
RIPLEY. Chronicon Mirabile, or Extracts from Parish Registers, 143. Chester MSS. in Coll. Arms, (Yorkshire,) ii. 175.
RIPPINGALE. Chester MSS. in Coll. Arms, (Lincolnshire,) i. 6.
RISBY. Chester MSS. in Coll. Arms, (Suffolk,) 333.
RISELEY. Blades' Genealogia Bedfordiensis, 240.
ROCHDALE. The Registers of the Parish Church of Rochdale, 1582-1641. Edited by Henry Fishwick. Rochdale, 1888-89. 8vo. 2 vols.
ROCHESTER CATHEDRAL. Chester MSS. in Coll. Arms, (Kent,) ii. 91.

ROMFORD. Notes and Queries, 3 S. ii 163; iii. 84. Chester MSS. in Coll. Arms, (Essex,) i. 145-232; ii. 63-95.

Roos. Register for the Parish of All Saints, Roos. Copied by R. B. Machell. Vol. i. Hull, 1888, 8vo.

ROPSLEY. Chester MSS. in Coll. Arms, (Lincolnshire,) i. 271.

ROTHERFIELD GREYS. Chester MSS. in Coll. Arms, (Oxfordshire,) ii. 173. MS. in Coll. Arms, J. P. cxcv. 61.

ROTHERHAM. Parish Register of Rotherham, 1542-1563. Historic Notices of Rotherham, by John Guest, 212-257. (Also printed separately.) British Museum, Add. MS. 24568.

ROTHWELL. Topography of Lofthouse, by G. Roberts, 91-96. Chester MSS. in Coll. Arms, (Yorkshire,) ii. 353.

ROTHWELL. Chester MSS. in Coll. Arms, (Northampton,) i. 107.

ROUSHAM. Chester MSS. in Coll. Arms, (Oxfordshire,) iii. 163.

ROXTON. Blades' Genealogia Bedfordiensis, 242.

ROXWELL. Chester MSS. in Coll. Arms, (Essex,) i. 23.

ROYSTON. Chronicon Mirabile, or Extracts from Parish Registers, 133. Chester MSS. in Coll. Arms, (Yorkshire,) ii. 339.

RUDGWICK. Chester MSS. in Coll. Arms, (Sussex,) i. 131-258.

RUSCOMBE. Chester MSS. in Coll. Arms, (Berkshire,) 127.

RUSHALL. The East Anglian, iv. 284.

RUSHTON. Chester MSS. in Coll. Arms, (Northampton,) i. 121.

RUSHTON. Chester MSS. in Coll. Arms, (Staffordshire,) 9.

RYTON. Chronicon Mirabile, or Extracts from Parish Registers, 61.

SADDLEWORTH. The Parish Registers of St. Chad, Saddleworth, 1613-1751. Edited by John Radcliffe. Uppermill, 1887, 8vo.

ST. ALBAN'S. Hare's Miscell. Par. Registers, MS. in Coll. Arms, 179.

    ,, ABBEY. Complete transcript, 1558-1689. Chester MSS. in Coll. Arms, (Herts,) i.

    ,, ST. PETER. Chester MSS. in Coll. Arms, (Herts,) ii. 135.

    ,, ST. MICHAEL. Chester MSS. in Coll. Arms, (Herts,) ii. 193.

    ,, ST. STEPHEN. Chester MSS. in Coll. Arms, (Herts,) ii. 195.

SAINTBURY. Excerpta ex Registris Parochialibus in Com. Gloucester. Middle Hill, 1854, fol.

ST. COLUMB MAJOR. The Registers of St. Columb Major, Cornwall, 1539-1780. Edited by A. J. Jewers. London, 1881, 8vo.

ST. DOMINICK. Heraldic Church Notes from Cornwall, by A. J. Jewers, 168.

ST. GERMANS. Heraldic Church Notes from Cornwall, by A. J. Jewers, 69-94.

ST. JOHNS'. Heraldic Church Notes from Cornwall, by A. J. Jewers, 13.

ST. OLAVE SOUTHWARK. Chester MSS. in Coll. Arms, (Surrey,) iii. 307-400; iv. 1-185.

ST. SAVIOUR SOUTHWARK. The Genealogist, New Series, vi. 145, 228.

St. Stephen's. Heraldic Church Notes from Cornwall, by A. J. Jewers, 97.

Saleby. Chester MSS. in Coll. Arms, (Lincolnshire,) i. 342.

Salehurst. Chester MSS. in Coll. Arms, (Sussex,) ii. 89.

Salford. Blades' Genealogia Bedfordiensis, 245.

Saltash. Heraldic Church Notes from Cornwall, by A. J. Jewers, 38.

Sandall. Chester MSS. in Coll. Arms, (Yorkshire,) ii. 347.

Sandbach. Chester MSS. in Coll. Arms, (Cheshire,) 167.

Sanderstead. Chester MSS. in Coll. Arms, (Surrey,) ii. 217-233.

Sandford. Chester MSS. in Coll. Arms, (Oxfordshire,) i. 53.

Sandford Orcas. Chester MSS. in Coll. Arms, (Somerset,) ii. 59 ; iii. 119.

Sandtoft. Register of the French Protestant Church at Sandtoft, 1642-1685. Yorkshire Archæological Journal, vii. 230-238.

Sandy. Blades' Genealogia Bedfordiensis, 246. Chester MSS. in Coll. Arms, (Bedfordshire,) 367.

Sarratt. Chester MSS. in Coll. Arms, (Herts,) ii. 199.

Sarsden. Chester MSS. in Coll. Arms, (Oxfordshire,) iii. 25.

Saxilby. Chester MSS. in Coll. Arms, (Lincolnshire,) i. 132.

Scampton. Chester MSS. in Coll. Arms, (Lincolnshire,) v. 303.

Scartho. Chester MSS. in Coll. Arms, (Lincolnshire,) iii. 408.

Scawby. Chester MSS. in Coll. Arms, (Lincolnshire,) i. 17.

Scotton. Chester MSS. in Coll. Arms, (Lincolnshire,) ii. 375.

Scotter. Chester MSS. in Coll. Arms, (Lincolnshire,) i. 208 ; v. 83.

Seaham. Chronicon Mirabile, or Extracts from Parish Registers, 76.

Seal. Chester MSS. in Coll. Arms, (Kent,) i. 93.

Seaton. (co. Rutland). The Genealogist, v. 61, 109.

Sedbergh. Extracts from Baptismal Register, 1606-1615. Printed on one side page only, 14 pp., 8vo.

Sedgberrow. Excerpta ex Registris Parochialibus in Com. Gloucester. Middle Hill, 1854, fol.

Sedgefield. Chronicon Mirabile, or Extracts from Parish Registers, 150.

Sedlescombe. Chester MSS. in Coll. Arms, (Sussex,) i. 41.

Seend. The Genealogist, iii. 387-398.

Semington. The Genealogist, New Series, vi. 118.

Selby. Morrell's History of Selby, 240-246.

Sempringham. Chester MSS. in Coll. Arms, (Lincolnshire,) ii. 168.

Sevenoaks. Chester MSS. in Coll. Arms, (Kent,) i. 97-122.

Shackerston. Parish Register, 1558-1630. Leicestershire Architectural Society's Transactions, v. 241. (The original is in the Bodleian Library.)

Shaftesbury, St. Peter. MS. in Coll. Arms, J. P. cxciii. 399.

Shalbourn. Chester MSS. in Coll. Arms, (Berkshire,) 105.

Shapwick. Chester MSS. in Coll. Arms, (Somerset,) i. 45.

Sharnbrook. Blades' Genealogia Bedfordiensis, 250. Harvey's Hundred of Willey, 476.

Shaugh Prior. Complete transcript, 1565-1887. MS. in Coll. Arms. 3 vols. fol.

SHAW. Chester MSS. in Coll. Arms, (Berkshire,) 109, 153.
SHEBBEAR. Complete transcript, 1576-1812. Chester MSS in Coll. Arms, (Devon,) v. 203-398.
SHEFFIELD. British Museum, Add. MS. 24471.
SHEFFIELD. A Register of Children baptized by the Rev. Mr. Jollie, 1681-1704. British Museum, Add. MS. 24436, fol. 74b. Yorkshire Notes and Queries, i. 80.
SHELFORD. Chester MSS. in Coll. Arms, (Notts,) ii. 69, 323.
SHELTON. Blades' Genealogia Bedfordiensis, 253.
SHELTON. (co. Norfolk.) The East Anglian, iv. 256.
SHEPTON MALLET. Chester MSS. in Coll. Arms, (Somerset,) i. 313.
SHERBORNE. Chester MSS. in Coll. Arms, (Dorset,) 75-160.
   „   ST. JOHN. Chester MSS. in Coll. Arms, (Hants,) 211.
SHERRINGTON. Chester MSS. in Coll. Arms, (Bucks,) 7.
SHEVIOCK. Heraldic Church Notes from Cornwall, by A. J. Jewers, 16.
SHILLINGTON. Blades' Genealogia Bedfordiensis, 255.
SHIPBORN. Chester MSS. in Coll. Arms, (Kent,) ii. 165.
SHIPDHAM. Chester MSS. in Coll. Arms, (Norfolk,) ii. 13-50.
SHIPTON SOLLERS. MS. in Coll. Arms, J. P. cxcii. 415.
SHIPTON OLIFFE. MS. in Coll. Arms, J. P. cxcii. 417.
SHOTTESBROOKE. The Genealogist, vii. 10.
SHREWSBURY, HOLY CROSS. Chester MSS. in Coll. Arms, (Shropshire,) 123.
SHUSTOKE. Chester MSS. in Coll. Arms, (Warwickshire,) 129.
SIBBERTOFT. Chester MSS. in Coll. Arms, (Northampton,) i. 135. MS. in Coll. Arms, R. B. G. xxiii. 135.
SIDMOUTH. MS. in Coll. Arms, J. P. cxcii. 244.
SILKSTON. Chester MSS. in Coll. Arms, (Yorkshire,) ii. 337.
SIXHILLS. Chester MSS. in Coll. Arms, (Lincolnshire,) ii. 252.
SKEGNESS. Chester MSS. in Coll. Arms, (Lincolnshire,) i. 154.
SKELLINGTHORPE. Chester MSS. in Coll. Arms, (Lincolnshire,) i. 277.
SLAUGHAM. Chester MSS. in Coll. Arms, (Sussex,) i. 259-272.
— SLEAFORD. Chester MSS. in Coll. Arms, (Lincolnshire,) ii. 191 ; v. 325.
SMARDEN. Haslewood's Memorials of Smarden, 231-237.
SNITTERTON. Hare's Miscell. Par. Registers, MS. in Coll. Arms, 139.
SNOWSHILL CHAPEL. Excerpta ex Registris Parochialibus in Com. Gloucester. Middle Hill, 1854, fol.
SOHAM. Hare's Miscell. Par. Registers, MS. in Coll. Arms, 141.
SOMERBY. Register of Somerby, 1601-1715. Leicestershire Architectural Society's Transactions, v. 273. The original is in British Museum, Add. MS. 24802.
SOMERBY. Chester MSS. in Coll. Arms, (Lincolnshire,) i. 265.
SOMERLEYTON. Chester MSS. in Coll. Arms, (Suffolk,) 299.
SOMERSAL-HERBERT. The Reliquary, xiv. 79.
SONNING. Chester MSS. in Coll. Arms, (Berkshire,) 95.
SOTBY. Chester MSS. in Coll. Arms, (Lincolnshire,) ii. 139.
SOULDROP. Blades' Genealogia Bedfordiensis, 259. Harvey's Hundred of Willey, 454.

SOUTH BERSTED. Chester MSS. in Coll. Arms, (Sussex,) i. 364; ii. 97.
SOUTH CADBURY. Chester MSS. in Coll. Arms, (Somerset,) i. 285.
SOUTH CARLTON. Chester MSS. in Coll. Arms, (Lincolnshire,) i. 130.
SOUTH ELKINGTON. Chester MSS. in Coll. Arms, (Lincolnshire,) i. 327.
SOUTHILL. Blades' Genealogia Bedfordiensis, 260.
SOUTHILL. Chester MSS. in Coll. Arms, (Notts.) ii. 335.
SOUTH HYKEHAM. Chester MSS. in Coll. Arms, (Lincolnshire,) ii. 122.
SOUTH KELSEY. Chester MSS. in Coll. Arms, (Lincolnshire,) v. 205.
SOUTH KYME. Chester MSS. in Coll. Arms, (Lincolnshire,) ii. 320 ; v. 341.
SOUTH LYNN. Chester MSS. in Coll. Arms, (Norfolk,) i. 219-248.
SOUTH LITTLETON. Chester MSS. in Coll. Arms, (Worcestershire,) 101.
SOUTH MARSTON. See STRATTON ST. MARGARET.
SOUTH MUSKHAM. Chester MSS. in Coll. Arms, (Notts,) ii. 76, 325.
SOUTH NEWINGTON. Chester MSS. in Coll. Arms, (Oxfordshire,) i. 157.
SOUTH OCKINGDON. Parish Registers, MS. in Coll. Arms, E. L. xi. 71.
SOUTH ORMSBY. Chester MSS. in Coll. Arms, (Lincolnshire,) i. 51.
SOUTH PETHERTON. Chester MSS. in Coll. Arms, (Somerset,) i. 103, 273.
SOUTH SHIELDS. Chronicon Mirabile, or Extracts from Parish Registers, 66.
SOUTH SOMERCOTES. Chester MSS. in Coll. Arms, (Lincolnshire,) iii. 383.
SOUTH THORESBY. Chester MSS. in Coll. Arms, (Lincolnshire,) i. 16.
SOUTHWARK. See ST. OLAVE, ST. SAVIOUR.
SOUTH WEALD. Registers of St. Peter's, South Weald, 1539-1573. Edited by Robert Hovenden. London, 1889, 8vo. Chester MSS. in Coll. Arms, (Essex,) iii. 379.
SOUTHWELL. Chester MSS. in Coll. Arms, (Notts,) i. 275-405.
SOUTH WESTON. Chester MSS. in Coll. Arms, (Oxfordshire,) ii. 199.
SOUTH WITHAM. Chester MSS. in Coll. Arms, (Lincolnshire,) ii. 107.
SPALDING. Chester MSS. in Coll. Arms, (Lincolnshire,) i. 83 ; v. 283.
SPANBY. Chester MSS. in Coll. Arms, (Lincolnshire,) ii. 154.
SPEEN. Chester MSS. in Coll. Arms, (Berkshire,) 229.
SPELSBURY. Chester MSS. in Coll. Arms, (Oxfordshire,) iii. 117.
SPILSBY. Chester MSS. in Coll. Arms, (Lincolnshire,) i. 160.
SPRINGTHORPE. Chester MSS. in Coll. Arms, (Lincolnshire,) i. 380.
SPROTBOROUGH. British Museum, Add. MSS. 24439, 24469.
SPROWSTON. Eastern Counties Collectanea, 14.
STAFFORD, ST. MARY. MS. in Coll. Arms, J. P. clxxxvii. 120.
STAGSDEN. Blades' Genealogia Bedfordiensis, 265. Harvey's Hundred of Willey, 136.
STAINDROP. Chronicon Mirabile, or Extracts from Parish Registers, 17.
STALBRIDGE. Chester MSS. in Coll. Arms, (Dorset,) 17.
STALLINGBOROUGH. Chester MSS. in Coll. Arms, (Lincolnshire,) v. 93.

STAMFORD, ST. GEORGE. The Reliquary, viii. 89, 151, 216. Chester MSS. in Coll. Arms, (Lincolnshire,) v. 153.

„ ST. JOHN. The Reliquary, xx. 233; xxi. 77, 157, 222; xxii. 53, 113; xxiv. 73.

„ ST. MARTIN. The Reliquary, xii. 51, 116; xiii. 165, 236. Chester MSS. in Coll. Arms, (Northampton,) i. 149.

„ ST. MARY. The Reliquary, ix. 113; x. 47; xi. 23, 173. Chester MSS. in Coll. Arms, (Lincolnshire,) v. 169.

„ ST. MICHAEL. The Reliquary, xiv. 41, 74, 231; xv. 39, 91, 170; xvi. 45, 75, 225; xvii. 88, 202; xviii. 95, 149, 212; xix. 46, 107, 166; xx. 40, 117. Chester MSS. in Coll. Arms, (Lincolnshire,) v. 243.

STANBRIDGE. Blades' Genealogia Bedfordiensis, 266.

STANBURY. Quaker Registers. Yorkshire Notes and Queries, i. 9-15.

STANDLAKE. Chester MSS. in Coll. Arms, (Oxfordshire,) iii. 95.

STANFORD (co. Northampton). Ass. Architectural Soc. Reports and Papers, xvii. 136-153.

STANFORD DINGLEY. Chester MSS. in Coll. Arms, (Berkshire,) 167.

STANHOPE. Chronicon Mirabile, or Extracts from Parish Registers, 80.

STANTON. Excerpta ex Registris Parochialibus in Com. Gloucester. Middle Hill, 1854, fol.

STANTON HARCOURT. MS. in Coll. Arms, J. P. cxcv. 111.

STANTON PRIOR. Chester MSS. in Coll. Arms, (Somerset,) ii. 189.

STANWAY. Collectanea Topographica et Genealogica, iv. 305.

STAPLEFORD (Notts). Miscellanea Genealogica et Heraldica, New Series, iii. 47.

STARTFORTH. Chronicon Mirabile, or Extracts from Parish Registers, 129.

STAUGHTON-PARVA. Blades' Genealogia Bedfordiensis, 267.

STAVELEY. British Museum, Add. MS. 24569.

STEBBING. Chester MSS. in Coll. Arms, (Essex,) ii. 21.

STEEPLE ASTON. Chester MSS. in Coll. Arms, (Oxfordshire,) i. 217.

STEEPLE BARTON. Chester MSS. in Coll. Arms, (Oxfordshire,) iii. 287.

STEEPLE BUMPSTED. Hare's Miscell. Par. Registers, MS. in Coll. Arms, 197.

STENIGOT. Chester MSS. in Coll. Arms, (Lincolnshire,) i. 165.

STEPPINGLEY. Blades' Genealogia Bedfordiensis, 269.

STEVENTON (Berks). Original Registers, 1556-1599. British Museum, Harleian MS. 2395.

STEVINGTON. Blades' Genealogia Bedfordiensis, 271. Harvey's Hundred of Willey, 165.

STEYNING. Chester MSS. in Coll. Arms, (Sussex,) i. 313.

STIFFORD. The Parish Register of Stifford, 1568-1783. Privately printed for F. A. Crisp, 1885, fol.

STILLINGTON. Complete transcript, 1666-1702. Chester MSS. in Coll. Arms, (Yorkshire,) ii. 133-166.

STOCK HARVARD. Registers of Stock Harvard, co. Essex, 1563-1700. Edited by Edward P. Gibson. London, 1881, 8vo.

STOCKPORT. Stockport Parish Registers, 1584-1620. By E. W. Bulkeley. Stockport, 1889, 4to. Chester MSS. in Coll. Arms, (Cheshire,) 339-362.

STOCKTON. Chronicon Mirabile, or Extracts from Parish Registers, 64.

STOCKTON. Hare's Miscell. Par. Registers, MS. in Coll. Arms, 175.

STOKE ABBAS. Chester MSS. in Coll. Arms, (Dorset,) 209.

STOKE D'ABERNON. MS. in Coll. Arms, J. P. cxciii, 320.

STOKE-SUB-HAMDON. Chester MSS. in Coll. Arms, (Somerset,) i. 263. MS. in Coll. Arms, J. P. cxciii. 404.

STOKE LYNE. Chester MSS. in Coll. Arms, (Oxfordshire,) i. 34.

STOKE NEWINGTON. William Robinson's History of Stoke Newington, 189-198.

STOKE ROCHFORD. Chester MSS. in Coll. Arms, (Lincolnshire,) ii. 327, 368; v. 345.

STONDON, UPPER. Blades' Genealogia Bedfordiensis, 273.

STOPHAM. Chester MSS. in Coll. Arms, (Sussex,) i. 31, 57.

STOTFOLD. Blades' Genealogia Bedfordiensis. 274.

STOUGHTON. Excerpta ex Registris Parochialibus in Com. Gloucester. Middle Hill, 1854, fol.

STOURTON (Wilts), 1570-1800. Edited by J. H. Ellis. Vol. xii. of the publications of the Harleian Society, Register Section.

STOW. Chester MSS. in Coll. Arms, (Lincolnshire,) i. 215.

STOWE-NINE-CHURCHES. Chester MSS. in Coll. Arms, (Northampton,) i. 95.

STOWELL. See HAMPNETT.

STRANTON. Chronicon Mirabile, or Extracts from Parish Registers, 6.

STRATFORD-ON-AVON. Excerpta ex Registris Parochialibus in Com. Gloucester. Middle Hill, 1854, fol. Chester MSS. in Coll. Arms, (Warwickshire,) 303. Parish Registers York, 64; a 4to. MS. in Coll. Arms.

STRATTON AUDLEY. Chester MSS. in Coll. Arms, (Oxfordshire,) i. 40.

STREATHAM. Collectanea Topographica et Genealogica, iii. 309. Chester MSS. in Coll. Arms, (Surrey,) iv. 287. MS. in Coll. Arms, J. P. cxciii. 310.

STREATLEY. Blades' Genealogia Bedfordiensis, 276.

STREET. Chester MSS. in Coll. Arms, (Somerset,) i. 253, 257.

STRETFORD. The Reliquary, xvii. 45, 93.

STRUBBY. Chester MSS. in Coll. Arms, (Lincolnshire,) i. 76.

STUBTON. The Registers of Stubton, co. Lincoln, 1577-1628. Printed at the private press of F. A. Crisp, 1883, fol.

STULHAM. Blades' Genealogia Bedfordiensis, 278.

STUDLAND. Chester MSS. in Coll. Arms, (Dorset,) 199.

STURMINSTER MARSHAL. MS. in Coll. Arms, J. P. cxcv. 72.

STUSTON. The East Anglian, iii. 60, 89, 249.

STUTTON. Some Account of the Parish of Stutton. By F. A. Crisp. London, 1881, fol., unpaged. Extracts from Registers at end.

SUDBROOKE. Chester MSS. in Coll. Arms, (Lincolnshire,) ii. 36.

SUDBURY, ALL SAINTS. Chester MSS. in Coll. Arms. (Suffolk,) 249.

SUFFIELD. Hare's Miscell. Par. Registers, MS. in Coll. Arms, 169.

SUNDERLAND. Chronicon Mirabile, or Extracts from Parish Registers, 16.
SUNDON. Blades' Genealogia Bedfordiensis, 279.
SUTTERTON. Chester MSS. in Coll. Arms, (Lincolnshire,) ii. 159 ; v. 223, 275.
SUTTON. Blades' Genealogia Bedfordiensis, 282.
SUTTON ST. JAMES. Chester MSS. in Coll. Arms, (Lincolnshire,) ii. 87.
SUTTON ST. NICHOLAS. The Genealogist, vii. 27.
SUTTON WALDRON. Nichols' Topographer, iii. 411.
SWAINSWICK. Annals of Swainswick, by R. E. M. Peach, 62-97.
SWALCLIFFE. Chester MSS. in Coll. Arms, (Oxfordshire,) iii. 153.
SWALLOW. Chester MSS. in Coll. Arms, (Lincolnshire,) ii. 312.
SWARBY. Chester MSS. in Coll. Arms, (Lincolnshire,) ii. 173.
SWARKESTON. Chester MSS. in Coll. Arms, (Derbyshire,) i. 91.
SWATON. Chester MSS. in Coll. Arms, (Lincolnshire,) ii. 212.
SWINBROOK. Chester MSS. in Coll. Arms, (Oxfordshire,) ii. 211.
SWINDERBY. Chester MSS. in Coll. Arms, (Lincolnshire,) ii. 203.
SWINESHEAD. Chester MSS. in Coll. Arms, (Lincolnshire,) i. 149 ; ii. 410; v. 215.
SWINHOPE. Chester MSS. in Coll. Arms, (Lincolnshire,) i. 40.
SWINSTEAD. Chester MSS. in Coll. Arms, (Lincolnshire,) i. 321.
SYDBURY. MS. in Coll. Arms, J. P. cxcii. 280.

TADDINGTON. The Reliquary, v. 87.
TALLINGTON. Chester MSS. in Coll. Arms, (Lincolnshire,) i. 397.
TANFIELD. Chronicon Mirabile, or Extracts from Parish Registers, 37.
TANNINGTON. The Parish Registers of Tannington, Suffolk, 1539-1714. Printed at the private press of F. A. Crisp, 1884, fol.
TATHWELL. Chester MSS. in Coll. Arms, (Lincolnshire,) i. 325.
TAUNTON, ST. JAMES. Chester MSS. in Coll. Arms, (Somerset,) i. 311.
    „   ST. MARY MAGDALEN. Chester MSS. in · Coll. Arms, (Somerset,) i. 55-94, 339.
TAXAL. Chester MSS. in Coll. Arms, (Cheshire,) 335.
TAYNTON. Chester MSS. in Coll. Arms, (Oxfordshire,) iii. 45.
TEALBY. Chester MSS. in Coll. Arms, (Lincolnshire,) iv. 133.
TEMPSFORD. Blades' Genealogia Bedfordiensis, 284.
TENDRING. Chester MSS. in Coll. Arms, (Essex,) i. 247.
TENTERDEN. Chester MSS. in Coll. Arms, (Kent,) ii. 1-75.
TETBURY. Gloucestershire Notes and Queries, i. 323. Chester MSS. in Coll. Arms, (Gloucestershire,) 321-340.
TEWIN. Chester MSS. in Coll. Arms, (Herts,) ii. 5.
THAME. F. G. Lee's History of Thame, 661. Chester MSS. in Coll. Arms, (Oxfordshire,) iii. 223.
THANET, ST. PETER'S. Parish Register of St. Peter's, Thanet, 1582-1777. Society of Antiquaries, MS.
THATCHAM. Chester MSS. in Coll. Arms, (Berkshire.) 155.
THEYDON GERNON. Chester MSS. in Coll. Arms, (Essex,) i. 241.

TREF EGLWYS. Baptisms, Burials, and Marriages, 1695-6. Privately printed by Sir T. Phillipps. Pp. 3, 12mo.

TRENT. Chester MSS. in Coll. Arms, (Somerset,) iii. 125.

TRENTHAM. Miscellanea Genealogica et Heraldica, 2nd Series, i. 111.

TRULL. Chester MSS. in Coll. Arms, (Somerset,) iii. 173.

TRUSTHORPE. Chester MSS. in Coll. Arms, (Lincolnshire,) i. 316.

TURKDEAN. Gloucestershire Notes and Queries, ii. 449.

TURVEY. Harvey's Hundred of Willey, 217. Blades' Genealogia Bedfordiensis, 304.

TWYFORD. Chester MSS. in Coll. Arms, (Hants,) 233.

TYDD ST. MARY. Chester MSS. in Coll. Arms, (Lincolnshire,) ii. 89.

UCKFIELD. Chester MSS. in Coll. Arms, (Sussex,) i. 15, 378.

UFFINGTON. Chester MSS. in Coll. Arms, (Lincolnshire,) i. 317.

UFTON COURT. Catholic Register of Ufton Court, Berkshire, and Woolhampton, 1741-1828. Privately printed for F. A. Crisp, 1889, fol.

ULCEBY. Chester MSS. in Coll. Arms, (Lincolnshire,) v. 113.

ULVERSTON. The Registers of Ulverston Parish Church, 1545-1812. By C. W. Bardsley and L. R. Ayre. Ulverston, 1886, 4to.

UPCHURCH. Original (Bishops') transcripts, 1612, 1661. British Museum, Add. MS. 32344.

UPTON. Chester MSS. in Coll. Arms, (Lincolnshire,) i. 204.

UPTON BISHOP. An Alphabetical List of all the Marriages, 1571-1883. Records of Upton Bishop, by Rev. F. T. Havergal, 26-41.

USSELBY. Chester MSS. in Coll. Arms, (Lincolnshire,) iv. 125.

UTTOXETER. Original (Bishops') transcripts, 1762-1766. British Museum, Add. MS. 32344.

WADDINGTON. Chester MSS. in Coll. Arms, (Lincolnshire,) ii. 233.

WADDINGHAM. Chester MSS. in Coll. Arms, (Lincolnshire,) ii. 16.

WADENHOE. Complete transcript. Chester MSS. in Coll. Arms, (Northampton,) ii. 57-116.

WADWORTH. British Museum, Add. MS. 24469.

WAKERLEY. Chester MSS. in Coll. Arms, (Northampton,) i. 229. MS. in Coll. Arms, R. B. G. xxiii. 135.

WALCOTT. Chester MSS. in Coll. Arms, (Lincolnshire,) i. 1.

WALESBY. Chester MSS. in Coll. Arms, (Lincolnshire,) v. 131.

WALPOLE ST. PETER. The East Anglian, iii. 167.

WALTHAM. Chester MSS. in Coll. Arms, (Lincolnshire,) iii. 388 ; iv. 109.

WALTHAM (co. Leicester). The Genealogist, New Series, iii. 252.

WALTHAM HOLY CROSS. Our Parish Registers, by W. Winters. Waltham Abbey, 1885, 8vo. (Contains extracts only.) Chester MSS. in Coll. Arms, (Essex,) iii. 363-378.

WALTHAMSTOW. Chester MSS. in Coll. Arms, (Essex,) iii. 221.

WALTON-ON-THE-HILL (Surrey). The Reliquary, x. 204.

WALTON-LE-WOLD. Chester MSS. in Coll. Arms, (Lincolnshire,) i. 28.

WANDSWORTH. The Registers of the Parish of Wandsworth, 1603-1787. By J. T. Squire. Lymington, 1889, 8vo.

WARDEN. Blades' Genealogia Bedfordiensis, 306.

WARDINGTON. Chester MSS. in Coll. Arms, (Oxfordshire,) iii. 57.

WARE. Chester MSS. in Coll. Arms, (Herts,) ii. 11.

WARGRAVE. Chester MSS. in Coll. Arms, (Berkshire,) 151.

WARMINGHURST. Chester MSS. in Coll. Arms, (Sussex,) i. 27, 376.

WARMINSTER. Chester MSS. in Coll. Arms, (Wilts,) 95.

WARNFORD. Chester MSS. in Coll. Arms, (Hants,) 195-209.

WARNHAM. Sussex Archæological Collections, xxxiii. 152-206. Chester MSS. in Coll. Arms, (Sussex,) i. 65-100.

WARPLESDON. MS. in Coll. Arms, J. P. cxciii. 300.

WARRINGTON. The First Vol. of Registers of Warrington, MS. in Warrington Museum and Library.

WARSOP. Warsop Parish Registers, by Richard J. King. Mansfield, 1884, 8vo. (Contains extracts only.)

WARSOP. Chester MSS. in Coll. Arms, (Notts,) ii. 51.

WARTON. Chester MSS. in Coll. Arms, (Lancashire,) 391-401.

WASHINGBOROUGH. Chester MSS. in Coll. Arms, (Lincolnshire,) i. 251 ; ii. 374.

WASHINGTON. Chronicon Mirabile, or Extracts from Parish Registers, 151.

WATERPERRY. Chester MSS. in Coll. Arms, (Oxfordshire,) i. 46.

WATERSTOCK. Chester MSS. in Coll. Arms, (Oxfordshire,) ii. 223.

WATFORD. Chester MSS. in Coll. Arms, (Herts,) ii. 203-217.

WATH. Nichols' Topographer, iii. 414.

WATLINGTON. Chester MSS. in Coll. Arms, (Oxfordshire,) iii. 67.

WATTON. Chester MSS. in Coll. Arms, (Herts.) ii. 125.

WEDMORE. Wedmore Parish Registers. Marriages, 1561-1839. Wells, 1888, 4to. The same : Burials, 1561-1860. Wells, 1890, 4to. The same : Baptisms, 1561-1812. Wells, 1890, 4to.

WEDNESBURY. Chester MSS. in Coll. Arms, (Staffordshire,) 133.

WELFORD. Chester MSS. in Coll. Arms, (Northampton,) i. 125.

WELLESBOURNE. Chester MSS. in Coll. Arms, (Warwickshire,) 71.

WELLINGBOROUGH. MS. in Coll. Arms, R. B. G. xxiii. 125.

WELLINGORE. Chester MSS. in Coll. Arms, (Lincolnshire,) i. 314.

WELLINGTON (Somerset). Humphreys' History of Wellington, 109.

WELLOW. Index to the Registers of Wellow, 1570-1887. By C. W. Empson. London, 1889, 8vo.

WELLS CATHEDRAL. MS. in Coll. Arms, R. B. G. xxiv. 1-15.

    „   ST. CUTHBERT. Chester MSS. in Coll. Arms, (Somerset,) i. 131.

WELWYN. Chester MSS. in Coll. Arms, (Herts,) ii. 141.

WENDLEBURY. Chester MSS. in Coll. Arms, (Oxfordshire,) iii. 301.

WERRINGTON. The Genealogist, iv. 61.

WEST ARDSLEY. Chester MSS. in Coll. Arms, (Yorkshire,) ii. 319.

WEST BARKWITH. Chester MSS. in Coll. Arms, (Lincolnshire,) i. 328.

WEST BROMWICH. Register of Baptisms and Burials, 1608-1616. West Bromwich Parish Magazine, May, 1879, and subsequent Numbers.

WESTBY. *See* BASSINGTHORPE.
WEST CHALLOW. Chester MSS. in Coll. Arms, (Berkshire,) 137.
WESTERHAM. Parochial History of Westerham, by G. L. Gower, 44-78.
WEST HALLAM. The Oldest Register of West Hallam, by Rev. C. Kerry. Reprinted from the Journal of the Derbyshire Archæological Society, 1887, 8vo., pp. 24.
WEST HAM. Chester MSS. in Coll. Arms, (Essex,) ii. 107-138.
WESTHAM. Chester MSS. in Coll. Arms, (Sussex,) i. 101 ; ii. 59.
WEST LAVINGTON. The Genealogist, New Series, iv. 68.
WESTLETON. East Anglian, iii. 311, 340.
WESTLEY. Chester MSS. in Coll. Arms, (Suffolk,) 331.
WESTMINSTER ABBEY. MS. in Coll. Arms, 'Registers, J. W.,' 1-37.
WEST MONKTON. Chester MSS. in Coll. Arms, (Somerset,) i. 295.
WESTON. Chester MSS. in Coll. Arms, (Lincolnshire,) ii. 42.
WESTON-ON-THE-GREEN. Chester MSS. in Coll. Arms, (Oxfordshire,) iii. 307.
WESTON SUBEDGE. Excerpta ex Registris Parochialibus in Com. Gloucester. Middle Hill, 1854, fol.
WESTON UNDERWOOD. Chester MSS. in Coll. Arms, (Bucks,) 36. Catholic Registers of Weston Underwood, 1710-1785. Privately printed for F. A. Crisp, 1887, fol.
WESTON. *See* ALCONBURY.
WELTONING. Blades' Genealogia Bedfordiensis, 313.
WEST QUANTOXHEAD. The Genealogist, ii. 24 ; iii. 26, 46.
WEST RASEN. Chester MSS. in Coll. Arms, (Lincolnshire,) iv. 149.
WEST TARRING. Chester MSS. in Coll. Arms, (Sussex,) i. 330. MS. in Coll. Arms, J. P. cxcii. 431.
WEST THEDDLETHORPE. Chester MSS. in Coll. Arms, (Lincolnshire,) i. 295.
WEST WICKHAM. Miscellanea Genealogica et Heraldica, New Series, iv. 393.
WETHERSFIELD. Chester MSS. in Coll. Arms, (Essex,) iii. 383.
WEYBRIDGE. *See* WOBURN LODGE.
WHAPLODE. Chester MSS. in Coll. Arms, (Lincolnshire,) ii. 51 ; v. 309.
WHAPLODE DROVE. Chester MSS. in Coll. Arms, (Lincolnshire,) ii. 54.
WHATFIELD. Chester MSS. in Coll. Arms, (Suffolk,) 293.
WHEATFIELD. Chester MSS. in Coll. Arms, (Oxfordshire,) ii. 231.
WHEATACRE BURGH. Hare's Miscell. Par. Registers, MS. in Coll. Arms, 149.
WHEATHAMPSTEAD. Chester MSS. in Coll. Arms, (Herts,) ii. 101.
WHICKHAM. Chronicon Mirabile, or Extracts from Parish Registers, 57.
WHIPSNADE. Blades' Genealogia Bedfordiensis, 315.
WHISSENDINE. The Genealogist, vii. 40.
WHISTON. British Museum, Add. MS. 24568.
WHITBURN. Chronicon Mirabile, or Extracts from Parish Registers, 28.

WHITBY. Chester MSS. in Coll. Arms, (Yorkshire,) ii. 273.
WHITCHURCH. British Museum, Add. MS. 24444.
WHITCHURCH. Chester MSS. in Coll. Arms, (Oxfordshire,) iii. 173.
WHITE WALTHAM. The Genealogist, vi. 49-57.
WHITTLESEY. Copies of 222 Marriage Registers from the Parish Book of St. Mary's Church, in Whittlesey, in the Isle of Ely, and County of Cambridge, 1662-1672. Published by James Coleman, 1880, 8vo., pp. 8.
WHITWORTH. Chronicon Mirabile, or Extracts from Parish Registers, 75.
WHIXLEY. Chester MSS. in Coll. Arms, (Yorkshire,) ii. 167.
WHORLTON. Chronicon Mirabile, or Extracts from Parish Registers, 83.
WICKENBY. Chester MSS. in Coll. Arms, (Lincolnshire,) ii. 175.
WICKERSLEY. British Museum, Add. MS. 24568.
WICKHAM. Chester MSS. in Coll. Arms, (Hants,) 149.
    ,, ST. PAUL. Chester MSS. in Coll. Arms, (Essex,) i. 253.
WIDECOMBE-IN-THE-MOOR. Chester MSS. in Coll. Arms, (Devon,) i. 249.
WIGAN. Chester MSS. in Coll. Arms, (Lancashire,) 197-222.
WIGGENHALL, ST. MARY MAGDALEN. Chester MSS. in Coll. Arms, (Norfolk,) i. 251.
WIGGINTON. Chester MSS. in Coll. Arms, (Oxfordshire,) ii. 237.
WIGTOFT. Chester MSS. in Coll. Arms, (Lincolnshire,) i. 368.
WILDEN. Blades' Genealogia Bedfordiensis, 317.
WILLINGHAM-BY-STOW. Chester MSS. in Coll. Arms, (Lincolnshire,) ii. 398.
WILLINGTON. Blades' Genealogia Bedfordiensis, 319.
WILLOUGHBY. Chester MSS. in Coll. Arms, (Lincolnshire,) i. 348.
WILLOUGHTON. Chester MSS. in Coll. Arms, (Lincolnshire,) i. 388.
WILMSLOW. Chester MSS. in Coll. Arms, (Cheshire,) 363.
WILSHAMSTEAD. Blades' Genealogia Bedfordiensis, 320.
WILTON. The Registers of Wilton, co. Somerset, 1558-1837, by J. H. Spencer. Taunton, 1890, 8vo.
WILTON-LE-WEAR. Chronicon Mirabile, or Extracts from Parish Registers, 87.
WINCKFIELD. Church Notes and Registers, MS. in Coll. Arms, 4.
WINDLESHAM. The Registers of Windlesham, Surrey. Baptisms, 1677-1783; Marriages, 1695-1753; Burials, 1695-1783. By W. U. S. Glanville-Richards. London, 1881, 8vo.
WINDSOR. Notes and Queries, 2 S. vi. 163, 239.
WINDSOR, NEW. Chester MSS. in Coll. Arms, (Berkshire,) 253.
WINTERTON. Chester MSS. in Coll. Arms, (Lincolnshire,) v. 373.
WINTHORPE. Chester MSS. in Coll. Arms, (Lincolnshire,) ii. 344, 404.
WINTRINGHAM. The entire register, 1558-1700. Chester MSS. in Coll. Arms, (Yorkshire,) i. 1-131.
WINWICK. Chester MSS. in Coll. Arms, (Lancashire,) 135-184.
WIRKSWORTH. Chester MSS. in Coll. Arms, (Derbyshire,) i. 29.
WISBECH. Copy of a Book containing Registers of Births, Burials,

and Marriages, etc., belonging to the General Baptist Church of Wisbech, Cambridgeshire. By W. Winkley. Harrow, 1860, 8vo.

WISBOROUGH GREEN. Chester MSS. in Coll. Arms, (Sussex,) ii. 1-35, 55.

WISPINGTON. Chester MSS. in Coll. Arms, (Lincolnshire,) ii. 135.

WISTASTON. Chester MSS. in Coll. Arms, (Cheshire,) 131.

WITHAM-ON-THE-HILL. Chester MSS. in Coll. Arms, (Lincolnshire,) i. 9.

WITHERN. Chester MSS. in Coll. Arms, (Lincolnshire,) ii. 33, 406.

WITTON-GILBERT. Chronicon Mirabile, or Extracts from Parish Registers, 35.

WIXFORD. See EXHALL.

WOBURN. Blades' Genealogia Bedfordiensis, 323. Church Notes and Registers, MS. in Coll. Arms, 10.

WOBURN LODGE CHAPEL. Catholic Registers of the Woburn Lodge Chapel and Weybridge, Surrey, 1750-1874. Printed for F. A. Crisp, 1888, fol.

WOKINGHAM. Chester MSS. in Coll. Arms, (Berkshire,) 87.

WOLD NEWTON. Chester MSS. in Coll. Arms, (Lincolnshire,) iv. 45.

WOLFARDISWORTHY. MS. in Coll. Arms, J. P. cxcii. 353.

WOLSINGHAM. Chronicon Mirabile, or Extracts from Parish Registers, 33

WOLSTON-CUM-BRANDON. The Genealogist, New Series, vi. 27.

WOLVERCOTE. See BRADFIELD.

WOMERSLEY. British Museum, Add. MS. 24169.

WOODBOROUGH. British Museum, Add. MS. 24592.

WOOLHAMPTON. See UFTON COURT.

WOOLWICH. Chester MSS. in Coll. Arms, (Kent,) i. 1-14.

WOOTTON. Blades' Genealogia Bedfordiensis, 327. Chester MSS. in Coll. Arms, (Bedfordshire,) 311, 363.

WOOTTON. Chester MSS. in Coll. Arms, (Lincolnshire), i. 197.

WOOTTON. Chester MSS. in Coll. Arms, (Oxfordshire,) ii. 249.

WORCESTER. Catholic Registers of the City of Worcester. Baptisms, 1685-1837. Privately printed for F. A. Crisp, 1887, fol.

WORKSOP. Chester MSS. in Coll. Arms, (Notts,) ii. 115-148.

WORMHILL. The Reliquary, iv. 237. Chester MSS. in Coll. Arms, (Derbyshire,) i. 21.

WORSBOROUGH. Chester MSS. in Coll. Arms, (Yorkshire,), ii. 245.

WRAGBY. Chester MSS. in Coll. Arms, (Lincolnshire,) ii. 180.

WRAXALL. Chester MSS. in Coll. Arms, (Somerset,) i. 1-24.

WRESTLINGWORTH. Blades' Genealogia Bedfordiensis, 331.

WRINGTON. Chester MSS. in Coll. Arms, (Somerset,) i. 299.

WYBERTON. Chester MSS. in Coll. Arms, (Lincolnshire,) v. 211.

WYMMINGTON. Blades' Genealogia Bedfordiensis, 333. Harvey's Hundred of Willey, 443.

YAPTON. Chester MSS. in Coll. Arms, (Sussex,) ii. 68.

YARBOROUGH. Chester MSS. in Coll. Arms, (Lincolnshire,) i. 121.

YARNTON. Chester MSS. in Coll. Arms, (Oxfordshire,) i. 89-136.

YATE. Parish Registers, Glouc., MS. in Coll. Arms, R. B. G. xxii. 126.

YATTENDEN. Parish Registers, MS. in Coll. Arms, E. L. xi. 14.

YATTON. Chester MSS. in Coll. Arms, (Somerset,) i. 165.

YAXLEY. The East Anglian, ii. 245.

YELDEN. Blades' Genealogia Bedfordiensis, 336.

YORK MINSTER. Burials, 1634-1836. The Yorkshire Archæological Journal, i. 226-330. Marriages, 1681-1762 ; ii. 97-128 ; iii. 81-146. Baptisms, 1686-1804 ; vi. 385-395. Parish Register, York, 64, a 4to. MS. in Coll. Arms.

„ ST. MARTIN CONEY STREET. Parish Register, York, 64, a 4to. MS. in Coll. Arms.

„ ST. HELEN. Parish Register, York, 64, a 4to. MS. in Coll. Arms.

„ ST. OLAVE. Parish Register, York, 64, a 4to. MS. in Coll. Arms.

„ ST. MICHAEL OUSEBRIDGE. Parish Register, York, 64, a 4to. MS. in Coll. Arms.

„ TRINITY MICKLEGATE. Parish Register, York, 64, a 4to. MS. in Coll. Arms.

„ ST. MICHAEL-LE-BELFREY. Parish Register, York, 64, a 4to. MS. in Coll. Arms.

„ ST. CRUX. Parish Register, York, 64, a 4to. MS. in Coll. Arms.

„ ST. CUTHBERT. Parish Register, York, 64, a 4to. MS. in Coll. Arms.

„ ST. MAURICE. Parish Register, York, 64, a 4to. MS. in Coll. Arms.

„ ST. MARY BISHOPHILL SENIOR. Chronicon Mirabile, or Extracts from Parish Registers, 147.

„ Extracts from Parish Registers within the City of York, and within the County of York. MS. in Coll. Arms, 2 vols., folio. The Parishes in the County of York in this collection are :—

Addle, near Leeds.	Fingall.	Sheriff Hutton.
Alne.	Garton.	Stillingfleet.
Barnburgh.	Hovingham.	Stokesley.
Batley.	Husthwaite.	Stonegrave.
Bolton Percy.	Kirkdale.	Strensall.
Bubwith.	Knaresborough.	Thirsk
Coxwold.	Nunnington.	Wensley.
Darfield.	Poppleton.	West Witton.
East Ardsley.	Ross.	Wintringham.
Escrick.	Sessay.	

„ A volume of entries from several parishes in the City of York, arranged alphabetically, in the handwriting of I. C. Brooke, and marked on the back ' $\frac{I}{R}$ Registers,' is in the College of Arms.

YOULGREAVE. The Reliquary, iv. 186. Chester MSS. in Coll. Arms, (Derbyshire,) i. 39.

MARRIAGE ALLEGATIONS.

DURHAM.

Durham Marriage Licences. MS in College of Arms, C. G. Y. clxxxvi. 106.

EXETER.

Marriage Licences of the Diocese of Exeter. Edited by Lieut.-Col. J. L. Vivian. Exeter, 1887-1889, 4to. *In progress.*

IRELAND.

Marriage Allegations in the Prerogative and Consistory Courts at Dublin, from earliest period to 1830. MS in possession of Henry Farnham Burke, Esq., Somerset Herald.
Marriage Licence Bonds from the Diocese of Killaloe, Ireland. British Museum, Add. MS 31883.

LEICESTER.

Extracts from Marriage Bonds of the Archdeaconry of Leicester. Leicestershire Architectural Society, vii. 168.

LICHFIELD.

Staffordshire Marriage Registers, Seventeenth Century. MS in the William Salt Library at Stafford. This is a collection of Lichfield Marriage Licences, 1660-1700.

LINCOLN.

Lincoln Marriage Licences, 1598-1628. Edited by A. Gibbons, London, 1888, 8vo.

LONDON.

Allegations for Marriage Licences, extracted by the late Col. J. L. Chester, LL.D., D.C.L. Harleian Society's Publications, vols. xxiii-xxvi. London, 1886-7, 8vo. The same collection has been published in a more convenient form, entitled :

London Marriage Licences, 1521-1869. Edited by Joseph Foster, from excerpts by the late Col. Chester, D.C.L. London, 1887, 8vo.

Allegations for Marriage Licences issued by the Vicar-General of the Archbishop of Canterbury, July, 1679—June, 1694. Edited by George J. Armytage. Harleian Society, vols. xxx. and xxxi. London, 1890, 8vo.

NOTTINGHAM.

Allegations for Marriage Licences granted in the Court of the Archdeacon of Nottingham, 1594-1732. MS in possession of George W. Marshall, Rouge Croix.

WORCESTER.

Marriage Licences in the Diocesan Registry at Worcester. By T. P. Wadley, M.A. Genealogist, vi. 177, 247, 316; vii. 89, 192, 199 ; New Series, i. 27, 102; ii. 52, 150, 212. A few copies of these Licences have been issued separately.

MS in Coll. Arms ; 'F. T. Church Notes,' iv. 237.

YORK.

Marriage Licences granted by the Ecclesiastical Court of York, 1567-1714. By William Paver. British Museum, Add. MSS 29651, 29667, 29668, 29670, 29671 *Index*. Partially printed in the Yorkshire Archaeological Journal, vii. 289, etc. But this print is of very little value, as the names are omitted in the indexes of the vols. in which the Allegations are printed.

Epitome of Marriage Licences granted by the Ecclesiastical Court of York, 1662-1714. MS in College of Arms. [By Wm. Paver.]

Extracts from Marriage Licences, which formerly belonged to Thomas Cotton of York, M.D., a dissenting minister. By William Paver. MS in College of Arms.

www.ingramcontent.com/pod-product-compliance
Lightning Source LLC
Chambersburg PA
CBHW021632270326
41931CB00008B/989